MACMILLAN / McGRAW-HILL

Teacher's READ-ALOUD ANTHOLOGY

Margaret H. Lippert
Anthologist

D1384646

As part of Macmillan / McGraw-Hill's effort to help make a difference to the environment, this anthology has been printed on recycled paper.

MACMILLAN / McGRAW-HILL SCHOOL PUBLISHING COMPANY
New York • Chicago • Columbus

The cover illustration, by Stefano Vitale, depicts a Mexican grandmother telling her grandchildren a story in their backyard. Typical of the folk art style in which it is rendered are the fanciful floating objects that surround the scene.

Macmillan/McGraw-Hill School Division
10 Union Square East
New York, New York 10003

Printed in the United States of America

ISBN 0-02-179118-X / 1

4 5 6 7 8 9   DBH   99 98 97 96 95 94 93

This book is dedicated to
you, the teacher, who will pick
the words of these stories up
off the page and send them
into the hearts and minds of
your students, and to you,
the listeners, who will take
the words and build them
into images.

MARGARET H. LIPPERT

Acknowledgments

The publisher gratefully acknowledges permission to reprint the following copyrighted material:

American Folklore Society
"Turkey Makes the Corn and Coyote Plants It" from "Tales of the White Mountain Apache" by Grenville Goodwin in MEMOIRS OF THE AMERICAN FOLKLORE SOCIETY, VOL. 33. Copyright © 1939 by the American Folklore Society. By permission of the American Folklore Society.

Atheneum Publishers
"Hen and Frog" from BEAT THE STORY-DRUM, PUM-PUM by Ashley Bryan. Copyright © 1980 Ashley Bryan. Reprinted with permission of Atheneum Publishers, an imprint of Macmillan Publishing Company.

Byrd Baylor
"How Our People Came To Be" and "Why Saguaros Grow on the South Side of the Hills" from AND IT IS STILL THAT WAY: *Legends told by Arizona Indian Children* with notes by Byrd Baylor. Copyright © 1976 by Byrd Baylor. Published by Trails West Press, Santa Fe, New Mexico. Reprinted by permission of Byrd Baylor.

Ellis Credle
"A Tall Turnip" from TALL TALES FROM THE HIGH HILLS by Ellis Credle. Copyright © 1957 by Ellis Credle. Reprinted by permission of the author.

Dial Books for Young Readers
"The Knee-High Man" from THE KNEE-HIGH MAN AND OTHER TALES by Julius Lester. Copyright © 1972 by Julius Lester. Used by permission of Dial Books for Young Readers, a division of Penguin Books USA Inc.

Dutton Children's Books
"Eeyore Has a Birthday and Gets Two Presents" from WINNIE-THE-POOH by A. A. Milne. Copyright 1926 by E. P. Dutton, renewed 1954 by A. A. Milne. Used by permission of Dutton Children's Books, a division of Penguin Books USA Inc.

Farrar, Straus and Giroux, Inc.
IT COULD ALWAYS BE WORSE by Margot Zemach. Copyright © 1976 by Margot Zemach. Reprinted by permission of Farrar, Straus and Giroux, Inc.

Harcourt Brace Jovanovich, Inc.
"The Wonderful Knapsack" from THIRTEEN DANISH TALES by Mary C. Hatch. Copyright 1947 by Harcourt Brace Jovanovich, Inc. and renewed 1975 by Edgun Wulff. Reprinted by permission of the publisher.

HarperCollins Publishers
"The Soup Stone" text from THE SOUP STONE by Maria Leach. Copyright 1954 by Funk & Wagnalls Company. Reprinted by permission of HarperCollins Publishers.

Melissa Heckler
"A House With a Star Inside." Copyright © 1991 by Melissa Heckler. Used with permission of the author.

Alfred A. Knopf, Inc.
"A Day When Frogs Wear Shoes" from MORE STORIES JULIAN TELLS by Ann Cameron. Text copyright © 1986 by Ann Cameron. Reprinted by permission of Alfred A. Knopf, Inc.

"A Wolf and Little Daughter" from THE PEOPLE COULD FLY: American Black Folktales told by Virginia Hamilton. Text copyright © 1985 by Virginia Hamilton. Reprinted by permission of Alfred A. Knopf, Inc.

Little, Brown and Company
"Jack and the Beanstalk" from FAVORITE FAIRY TALES TOLD AROUND THE WORLD, retold by Virginia Haviland. Text copyright © 1959 by Virginia Haviland. By permission of Little, Brown and Company.

CONTENTS

Introduction   10

🔊 **Squirrel's Song**
a Hopi tale told by Diane Wolkstein
Read-Aloud Time: 7-10 minutes
(for **Down By the Bay**)   16

The Knee-High Man
an American black folk tale retold by Julius Lester
Read-Aloud Time: 3-5 minutes
(for **The Chick and the Duckling**)   21

Grandfather Bear is Hungry
an Eiven folk tale from Russia
retold by Margaret Read MacDonald
Read-Aloud Time: 3-5 minutes
(for **My Friends**)   23

🔊 **Hen and Frog**
a Hausa tale from Nigeria retold by Ashley Bryan
Read-Aloud Time: 12-15 minutes
(for **Rain**)   26

🔊 **La Hormiguita**
a tale from Spanish New Mexico retold by Joe Hayes
Read-Aloud Time: 7-10 minutes
(for **One Monday Morning**)   32

The Owl and the Pussy-Cat
a poem by Edward Lear
Read-Aloud Time: 2-4 minutes
(for **Together**)   36

How Our People Came to Be and
Why Saguaros Grow on the South Side of Hills
legends told by Arizona Indian children to Byrd Baylor
Read-Aloud Time: 3-5 minutes
(for **Everything Grows**)   37

🔊 = *available on audiocassettes*

Turkey Makes the Corn and Coyote Plants It
a White Mountain Apache tale
retold by Richard Erdoes and Alfonso Ortiz
Read-Aloud Time: 7-10 minutes
(for **Bet You Can't**)   39

Kanji-jo, the Nestlings
a Mende folk tale from West Africa
retold by Margaret Read MacDonald
Read-Aloud Time: 9-12 minutes
(for **Whose Baby?**)   42

The Emperor's New Clothes
a Danish fairy tale by Hans Christian Andersen
adapted by Amy Ehrlich
Read-Aloud Time: 9-12 minutes
(for **You'll Soon Grow into Them, Titch**)   51

Little Red Riding Hood
a German folk tale retold by Margaret H. Lippert
Read-Aloud Time: 5-7 minutes
(for **Coco Can't Wait**)   55

The Wonderful Knapsack
a Danish folk tale retold by Mary C. Hatch
Read-Aloud Time: 12-15 minutes
(for **I Need a Lunch Box**)   58

The Fox Went Out on a Chilly Night
an American ballad
Singing Time: 3-5 minutes
(for **Hattie and the Fox**)   64

The Foolish, Timid Rabbit
a Jataka tale from India retold by Ellen C. Babbitt
Read-Aloud Time: 4-7 minutes
(for **The Story of Chicken Licken**)   66

A Tall Turnip
an Appalachian tall tale collected by Ellis Credle
Read-Aloud Time: 5-7 minutes
(for **The Great Big Enormous Turnip**)   69

The Old Woman Who Lost Her Dumplings
a Japanese fairy tale retold by Lafcadio Hearn
Read-Aloud Time: 7-10 minutes
(for **The Missing Tarts**)   72

The Squeaky Door
a Puerto Rican folk tale adapted by Laura Simms
Read-Aloud Time: 10-13 minutes
(for **The Bed**)   76

A Wolf and Little Daughter
an American black folk tale told by Virginia Hamilton
Read-Aloud Time: 3-5 minutes
(for **The Gunnywolf**)   79

Jack and the Beanstalk
an English fairy tale retold by Virginia Haviland
Read-Aloud Time: 13-16 minutes
(for **In the Attic**)   82

Why Leopard Has Black Spots
a story from the Dan people of Liberia
told by Won-Ldy Paye
edited by Margaret H. Lippert
Read-Aloud Time: 7-10 minutes
(for **The Trek**)   88

The Black Cat
an American folk tale retold by Margaret H. Lippert
Read-Aloud and Drawing Time: 5-10 minutes
(for **The Line Sophie Drew**)   93

The Elves and the Shoemaker
a German fairy tale by the Brothers Grimm
adapted by Amy Ehrlich
Read-Aloud Time: 5-7 minutes
(for **Jimmy Lee Did It**)   100

A Day When Frogs Wear Shoes
a story by Ann Cameron
Read-Aloud Time: 8-11 minutes
(for **Henry and Mudge in Puddle Trouble**)   102

The Soup Stone
a Belgian folk tale retold by Maria Leach
Read-Aloud Time: 4-7 minutes
(for **Eat Up, Gemma**)   108

The City Mouse and the Country Mouse
a fable by Aesop
Read-Aloud Time: 4-7 minutes
(for **Guinea Pigs Don't Read Books**)   111

How the Stars Came to Be
*a story adapted from several Native American tales
by Lynn Moroney*
Read-Aloud Time: 6-9 minutes
(for **Baby Rattlesnake**)   113

It Could Always Be Worse
a Yiddish folk tale retold by Margot Zemach
Read-Aloud Time: 7-10 minutes
(for **Fortunately**)   116

Eeyore Has a Birthday and Gets Two Presents
from Winne-the-Pooh *by A. A. Milne*
Read-Aloud Time: 15-20 minutes
(for **A Birthday Basket for Tía**)   119

A House with a Star Inside
a story retold by Melissa Heckler
Read-Aloud Time: 7-10 minutes
(for **Mr. Rabbit and the Lovely Present**)   128

The Tale of the Tales
a Russian folk tale by George and Helen Papashvily
Read-Aloud Time: 3-5 minutes
(for **A Letter to Amy**)   131

Notes About the Authors and Storytellers   133

Indexes of Origins, Authors, and Titles   136

$\mathscr{I}$NTRODUCTION

by Margaret H. Lippert

Long before I wrote stories, I listened for stories. Listening for them is something more acute than listening to them. I suppose it's an early form of participation in what goes on. Listening children know stories are there. When their elders sit and begin, children are just waiting and hoping for one to come out, like a mouse from its hole.

EUDORA WELTY[1]

This book is stuffed with mice. Your students are waiting.

You are part of a long tradition of storytellers and story readers. Stories belong to us all. From ancient times, people have been entertained and nourished by stories. All of us in our own families and culture have, like Eudora Welty, been entranced by the tales that have been told to us from the time we first started to listen. From these stories, we learned about listening and speaking and then about reading—connecting the images and messages of stories with print and with books.

The power of stories draws us to ideas and thoughts and feelings that we want and need to explore. Through stories we learn about the experiences of others and come to understand ourselves better. The best stories take us from where we are and lead us, word by word, image by image, into places known and unknown, familiar and new, comfortable and exciting.

Reading aloud opens students to a new way of learning—listening. Many of us, and many of our students, are unaccustomed to listening carefully. We tune out much of what goes on around us. We need to remember the power of listening and help our students do the same.

Reading aloud can grip students in a listening vise—because they want to know what will happen next, they listen with fully focused attention. Since students can understand a much larger vocabulary than they can read themselves, when we read aloud we expose them to more sophisticated concepts and content than they could read independently. People of traditional cultures knew this—they passed on knowledge through their stories.

As you read aloud, you give your students stories and something of yourself. You build a community in your classroom that links you and your students to one another, to the story, and to the thinking and feeling of the author and the culture from which that story springs. Your students stretch and grow, discovering the pathways and journeys of others and, in the process, making discoveries of their own.

A READ-ALOUD CELEBRATION

Each Read Aloud in this collection relates in some way—theme, style, author, content—to a selection in the Macmillan/McGraw-Hill Reading/Language Arts student anthologies. Many of the Read Alouds are traditional tales, stories that were handed down from one generation to another within a particular culture. Traditional stories include folk tales, fairy tales, myths, legends, tall tales, and fables. In addition to traditional literature, classics and contemporary literature are represented. Since stories come in many forms, a narrative poem and a ballad have been integrated into the collection as well.

In order to root this collection in the traditional oral heritage from which stories spring, I interviewed people who grew up in storytelling cultures and taped them telling stories so that you and your students would have access to their wisdom and to their stories. Some of these gifted storytellers are included on the SONGS AND STORIES AUDIOCASSETTES that are offered with the series.

The information about the contributors and the indexes at the end of the collection provide important information for you to share with your students about the origins of the tales and of the tellers.

HINTS FOR EFFECTIVE READING ALOUD

It is preferable, though not absolutely necessary, to skim through a story before you read it aloud. That way you will know where the story is headed, and you can adjust your reading style to the mood and rhythm of the story.

As you read, take your time and read with involvement and intensity. Your students will need time to construct story images and to process ideas as the story moves along. To help you judge the time you will need to allow for each story reading, the range of times it took several different teachers to read each story aloud to a group of students is included in the CONTENTS.

Sometimes questions will arise in response to a story. When this happens, I often ask students if they can answer the questions that have been raised. I have done this countless times, and, no matter how difficult the question, no student has ever said, "I don't know." Within the story's context, they do know, and they help one another explore the answers to their own questions.

Now I often ask after reading or telling a story, "Was there any part of the story that was unclear to you?" or "What did you wonder about as you listened to the story?" There are always many questions. And frequently there are many answers to a question. The harder the question, the more ideas and responses the question seems to generate. For example, after hearing me tell *Yeh-Shen*,[2] which is a Chinese version of the Cinderella story, one third grader asked, "Why did the stepmother kill the fish?" Seven children offered seven different explanations. Some of the responses were as follows: "Maybe she didn't like the fish." "One of the reasons could be that she wanted the meat from the fish. Or that she didn't want the girl [Yeh-Shen] to be friends with the fish." "I think she was just plain mean."

The students listened to the story. They struggled with parts that were unclear or unexplained, and they integrated all of their previous knowledge with the information generated in the story. They also developed plausible explanations to justify the actions of the characters and the events in the story.

In an atmosphere where questions are encouraged, hard questions are more likely to rise to the surface so they can be explored. Every question is a new starting point. Through ALL their questions, students seek meaning and struggle collaboratively to find answers to their own puzzling questions about the stories. What a wonderful model for seeking responses to the puzzling questions that confront them in their lives.

"I DO AND I UNDERSTAND"

There is an ancient Chinese proverb: "I hear and I forget. I see and I remember. I do and I understand."

By reading these stories aloud, you make them part of the oral tradition. Just listening to these stories will enrich the imaginations of your students, offering them new ideas and insights. But if your students re-create a favorite story in another form, it will become theirs in an even deeper way. "Doing" the stories leads to further understanding and appreciation of them.

Your students may wish to retell the story as a group in their own words, or to illustrate or depict the story in paintings, collages, or dioramas. They may enjoy spontaneously reenacting the story without props or scenery, or perhaps with the simplest of these. They may choose to write their favorite or least favorite part of the story, or their own version of the story either in whole or in part. If they do any of these things, either prompted by you or motivated on their own, they will know the story more intimately. The better they know the story, the more comfortable they will feel with it, and the better they will like it. The more they like it, the more they will want to share it, perhaps even outside the classroom, with family or friends. Thus the oral tradition continues.

ONWARD TO STORYTELLING

As a storyteller and story lover, I would be remiss if I did not encourage you to try telling, without the text, a tale or two. Telling a story is fun. It also models for students the possibility that they, too, can recall, retell, and enjoy stories whenever they wish. If you've told stories before, you know the flexibility and closeness engendered by direct contact with listeners, without an intervening page. If you haven't, you could begin with a short, familiar tale.

13

You don't need to memorize the words to enjoy telling stories. In fact, memorizing the words may distract you from the images and sequence of the tale itself. I simply picture the story as it takes place, then describe it to my listeners as I "see" it. This is the same skill you use when relating an anecdote that happened to you or when telling a joke. As a teacher, you already know how to hold the attention of your class. Storytelling is one small step beyond explaining a concept or describing an assignment.

The author-storyteller-artist Ashley Bryan has a favorite African proverb: "He who learns, teaches!" Learn the craft of storytelling along with your students. Allow them to watch you struggle and try and learn. Make mistakes and work through your mistakes. Allow them also to watch you as you succeed and soar on the wings of new stories. This will teach them about your love of story and language, and about how much you are willing to risk for them.

ENDINGS AND BEGINNINGS

From here, it is up to you. The stories are yours now. Read them, enjoy them, pass them along. By sharing these stories with your students, you will preserve them for at least one more generation.

Since this is a book of stories, I'd like to end this introduction with a story, or to be more accurate, a part of a Russian folk tale that is my favorite story. The oldest man in the village, encouraging a young boy to tell his first story to the expectant listeners around the fire, says:

> *A story is a letter that comes to us from yesterday.*
> *Each person who tells it adds his word to the message and*
> *sends it on to tomorrow. So begin.*
>
> from "The Tale of the Tales"[3]

[1]Eudora Welty, *One Writer's Beginnings* (Cambridge, MA: Harvard University Press, 1983), p. 16.

[2]Ai-Ling Louie, *Yeh-Shen: A Cinderella Story from China* (New York: Philomel Books, 1982).

[3]George and Helen Papashvily, "The Tale of the Tales," *Yes and No Stories: A Book of Georgian Folk Tales* (New York: Harper & Brothers, 1946).

I can promise that once you begin the daily experience of reading aloud to children, it will become one of the best parts of your day and the children's day, minutes and hours that will be treasured for years to come.

JIM TRELEASE
from *The Read-Aloud Handbook*

SQUIRREL'S SONG

a Hopi tale told by Diane Wolkstein

Long before dawn Squirrel jumped down from his nest in the cottonwood tree and scampered over the hill to Chipmunk's house.

"Chipmunk, are you awake?" Squirrel called softly.

No answer.

"Chipmunk," Squirrel called louder. "Are you ready?"

"I'm coming, Squirrel," Chipmunk yawned, opening one eye and shaking himself awake. "I'm coming."

Soon Chipmunk and Squirrel were racing along the gully on their way to the peach orchard. "*Chhh-t*, slow down," Squirrel said. "We're coming near the peaches." The two friends crept quietly up to the orchard and hid behind the trees.

They saw the old Hopi who guarded the orchard watering one of the peach trees. They waited and waited, and finally the old man went to the river to bring back more water.

Then they ran into the orchard and took turns climbing the trees and knocking down the peaches. They picked the sweetest, plumpest peaches and carried them to a flat rock overlooking the mesa.

Squirrel opened the peaches. He gave Chipmunk the flesh and kept the kernel for himself. They ate peach after peach and

16

watched the sun fill the mesa with soft yellow light. When the rock became too hot, Squirrel and Chipmunk went to sit in the coolness of its shadow. Chipmunk hummed little tunes to himself while Squirrel dozed off to sleep.

That afternoon as they were on their way home, Chipmunk was still humming. Suddenly, Squirrel stopped and said:

"Chipmunk, you sing so well. Why don't you make a song?"

"What kind of song?"

"A song for eating peaches. Then when we eat peaches, we can sing and have a song to dance to."

"Let me try," said Chipmunk.

All day and all night Chipmunk worked on a song. When Squirrel came in the morning, Chipmunk was waiting for him.

"The song is ready," he said, "and it's about more than peaches. It's about you. Listen." He sang it twice:

> *Squirrel cries*
> *Kree-kree Kree-kree*
> *Eating peaches*
> *Climbing trees.*
>
> *Squirrel cries*
> *Kree-kree Kree-kree*
> *Eating peaches*
> *Climbing trees.*

But to Chipmunk's amazement, Squirrel did not like the song. In fact he was angry.

"Why did you song-tie me?" Squirrel asked angrily. "Now everyone will know all about me."

17

"That's what a song does," Chipmunk explained. "A song tries to catch you."

"But I don't want to be caught," Squirrel said. "I don't want to be caught by the old man in the orchard and I don't want to be caught by your song."

"Oh, Squirrel, a song can't *really* catch you. Anyhow, it's your song. You can change it."

"I never thought of that," said Squirrel. "I never had a song of my own before. Sing it again, Chipmunk."

Chipmunk sang Squirrel's song:

> *Squirrel cries*
> *Kree-kree Kree-kree*
> *Eating peaches*
> *Climbing trees.*
>
> *Squirrel cries*
> *KREE-KREE KREE-KREE*
> *Eating peaches*
> *Climbing trees.*

The third time, Squirrel joined in. He was beginning to like his song. He sang the "kree-kree's" very loudly. They practiced the song over and over and sang it the whole way to the peach orchard.

Just as they arrived, they saw the old Hopi leaving for the river. So they rushed into the orchard, knocked down lots of peaches, and carried them to the flat rock.

Then they began to dance. They skipped about on their hind legs and waved their front legs. Squirrel turned somersaults

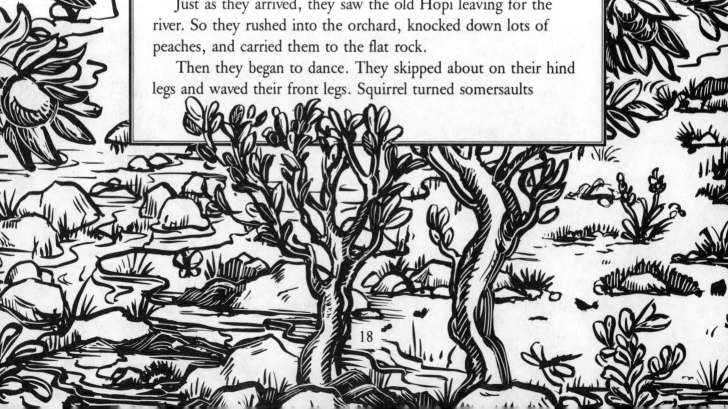

backwards and forwards. Chipmunk did cartwheels. The sun's rays darted across the mesa. They forgot everything but their song. They danced faster and faster and sang louder and louder:

> SQUIRREL CRIES
> KREE-KREE KREE-KREE
> EATING PEACHES
> CLIMBING TREES.

They sang so loudly they did not hear the old man returning from the river.

They did not hear his footsteps as he tiptoed up to the flat rock and saw Squirrel and Chipmunk and all the peaches scattered about.

"So!" he shouted. "It's you two who have been eating the peaches!"

Whssst! Chipmunk and Squirrel were off. They ran as fast as they could to Chipmunk's house and dove in.

But the old man ran right after them and stood with his feet planted over Chipmunk's house.

"I know where you are now," he said, "and I'm not moving until you come out."

"What are we going to do?" whispered Chipmunk. "It's all my fault, Squirrel. I should never have made such a song."

"No," said Squirrel. "I'm glad I have a song. But you only caught part of me in that song. Now watch me!"

Whssst! Squirrel jumped out of the hole and dashed between the legs of the old man. *Whhhht!* The old man was so surprised he tumbled over and landed on his bottom. By the time he got up, Squirrel was far away.

Chipmunk peeked out of the hole and saw the old man chasing after Squirrel. But Squirrel was going so fast that after a while the old man became too tired and went back to the orchard.

The next morning Squirrel arrived at Chipmunk's house as usual.

"Chipmunk," he called softly. "Are you awake?"

"I'm ready, Squirrel, and so is your song. It's bigger now. Listen:"

> *Squirrel cries*
> *Kree-kree Kree-kree*
> *Eating peaches*
> *Climbing trees.*
>
> *Squirrel runs*
> *Kwik-kwik Kwik-kwik*
> *Squirrel goes fast*
> *Lickety-split.*

"The song *is* bigger," Squirrel agreed. "But it will have to keep growing if it's going to catch me."

Squirrel was off to the peach orchard, and Chipmunk, too. But Chipmunk had to run fast to keep up with Squirrel, for Squirrel was going faster than ever.

The Knee-High Man

an American black folk tale retold by Julius Lester

Once upon a time there was a knee-high man. He was no taller than a person's knees. Because he was so short, he was very unhappy. He wanted to be big like everybody else.

One day he decided to ask the biggest animal he could find how he could get big. So he went to see Mr. Horse. "Mr. Horse, how can I get big like you?"

Mr. Horse said, "Well, eat a whole lot of corn. Then run around a lot. After a while you'll be as big as me."

The knee-high man did just that. He ate so much corn that his stomach hurt. Then he ran and ran and ran until his legs hurt. But he didn't get any bigger. So he decided that Mr. Horse had told him something wrong. He decided to go ask Mr. Bull.

"Mr. Bull? How can I get big like you?"

Mr. Bull said, "Eat a whole lot of grass. Then bellow and bellow as loud as you can. The first thing you know, you'll be as big as me."

So the knee-high man ate a whole field of grass. That made his stomach hurt. He bellowed and bellowed and bellowed all day and all night. That made his throat hurt. But he didn't get any bigger. So he decided that Mr. Bull was all wrong too.

Now he didn't know anyone else to ask. One night he heard Mr. Hoot Owl hooting, and he remembered that Mr. Owl knew everything. "Mr. Owl? How can I get big like Mr. Horse and Mr. Bull?"

"What do you want to be big for?" Mr. Hoot Owl asked.

"I want to be big so that when I get into a fight, I can whip everybody," the knee-high man said.

Mr. Hoot Owl hooted. "Anybody ever try to pick a fight with you?"

The knee-high man thought a minute. "Well, now that you mention it, nobody ever did try to start a fight with me."

Mr. Owl said, "Well, you don't have any reason to fight. Therefore, you don't have any reason to be bigger than you are."

"But, Mr. Owl," the knee-high man said, "I want to be big so I can see far into the distance."

Mr. Hoot Owl hooted. "If you climb a tall tree, you can see into the distance from the top."

The knee-high man was quiet for a minute. "Well, I hadn't thought of that."

Mr. Hoot Owl hooted again. "And that's what's wrong, Mr. Knee-High Man. You hadn't done any thinking at all. I'm smaller than you, and you don't see me worrying about being big. Mr. Knee-High Man, you wanted something that you didn't need."

GRANDFATHER BEAR
IS
HUNGRY

an Eiven folk tale from Russia
retold by Margaret Read MacDonald

In the spring, when the warm sun began to shine on Bear's cave,
Bear woke up and came out into the sunshine.
Ohhhhhh. . . . He felt . . . HUNGRY!

Bear had not eaten a thing all winter long.
"I am so HUNGRY!" growled Bear.
"I am so HUNGRY!"

Bear lumbered down to the berry patch.
It was early in the spring.

The berries were not ripe yet.
"I am so HUNGRY!" roared Bear.
"I am so HUNGRY!"

Bear galumped down to the stream.
It was too early in the spring.
The salmon were not running yet.
"I am so HUNGRY!" howled Bear.
"I am so HUNGRY!"

Bear stormed back into the forest.
He began to claw at a rotten tree stump.

23

But he could not find a single grub inside the stump.
"I am so HUNGRY!"
"I am so HUNGRY!"

Bear sat down.
He put his nose between his paws and he began to moan.
"I am so HUNGRY!"
"I am so HUNGRY!"

Tiny Chipmunk,
who lived under the stump,
came scurrying out to see what was making such a commotion.

"Grandfather Bear!
What is wrong?
Why are you moaning so loudly?"

Grandfather Bear looked at the tiny animal.

"I haven't eaten all winter and . . .
    I am so HUNGRY!"

Chipmunk cocked his head to one side and thought.
"I still have nuts and berries stored away in my burrow,
    Grandfather Bear.
I will share them with you!"
Chipmunk disappeared down his hole.
In a moment he was back with his cheeks full of nuts and
    berries.
Chipmunk dropped them in front of Grandfather Bear.

"HUNGRY!" said Grandfather Bear
and lapped up the little pile of nuts and berries.

Chipmunk ran back into his hole.
Back and forth
back and forth
Chipmunk ran,
carrying load after load of nuts and berries for Grandfather
    Bear.
His food was tiny, but gradually Grandfather Bear became full.

"Thank you, Chipmunk," said Grandfather Bear.
"You are a very small animal.
But you are kind."

Grandfather Bear reached out his huge paw.
He gently stroked his claws across the trembling back of
    the little chipmunk.
And where the claws passed
five black lines were left.

"Now you are handsome,"
    said Grandfather Bear.
"Whenever anyone sees you, Chipmunk,
they will notice your stripes,
and they will remember your kind heart."

And so it is even today.
When you see tiny Chipmunk scurrying about
with his fine black stripes,
you will remember his kindness to Grandfather Bear.

HEN AND FROG

a Hausa tale from Nigeria retold by Ashley Bryan

I'VE TOLD ONE TALE, HERE'S ANOTHER
CALL YOUR SISTER, CALL YOUR BROTHER.

Frog and Hen once met. They walked along together.

Hen strut two steps, pecked at a bug.

Frog bopped three hops, flicked his tongue at a fly.

Strut two steps, peck at a bug.

Bop three hops, flick at a fly.

Hen flapped her wings and spun around. Frog slapped his legs and tapped the ground.

"All in together now," clucked Hen.

"How do you like the weather now?" croaked Frog.

"O click clack," clucked Hen. "See that dark cloud? That's a sign, I know it. A storm's coming."

Strut two steps, peck at a bug.

"It's still a way far off," said Frog.

Bop three hops, flick at a fly.

"Good!" said Hen. "Then there's time. Frog, let's make a hut before the storm hits."

"A hut? Not me!" said Frog. "Here's a neat hole. I'm going to get into that. Uh-uh, I won't help you make a hut."

"Suit yourself," said Hen. "If you won't help me, then I'll make the hut myself."

Hen set to work and Frog jumped into the hole. While Hen worked, Frog sang:

"Kwee kwo kwa
Kwa kwo kwee
A hole in the ground
Is a hut to me."

Hen was a skillful hut builder. She flipped and she flapped, pieced, pecked and pulled every branch and straw into place. She put in two windows, a door, and thatched the roof, leaving a space in the middle for the smoke of the fireplace.

"Click, clack, cluck," she sang. "Click, clack, cluck, claa, clee."

The dark cloud came closer.

"Quick Frog," said Hen, "there's still time. Help me make a bed for the hut."

Frog sang:

"Kwee kwo kwa
  Kwa kwo kwee
  The ground in the hole
  Is a bed to me."

"Well!" said Hen. "If you won't help me, then I'll make the bed myself."

So Hen built the bed all by herself. She lay down to test it.

"O click clack cluck," she sang, "click, clack, cluck, claa, clee."

The dark cloud came even closer.

"Frog," said Hen, "there's still a little time left before the storm hits. Help me gather corn."

Frog sang:

"Kwee kwo kwa
  kwa kwo kwee
  The bugs in the hole
  Are food to me."

"Uh-uh," said Hen. "If you won't help me, then I'll gather the corn myself."

So Hen gathered the corn all by herself. She piled it by the fireplace and then rolled some pumpkins onto the thatched roof. She ran into her hut and latched the door just as the storm broke.

Blam-bam-pa-lam! Blam-bam-pa-lam!

The thunder rolled, the earth shook, tree branches tossed, and Frog was jostled in his hole.

"Kwa kwee," he sang, "kwee kwaaa!"

The rain came down, it really poured. Hen went to the window and looked out. Frog was standing up in his hole, swaying and singing a riddle song:

"Her children dance madly
  Mama never dances
  Riddle me this, riddle me that,
  Riddle me 'round the answers.
  Mama is a tree trunk
  Her children are the branches."

"Fool," said Hen. "This is no time for riddles."

27

Frog stamped as he sang. Suddenly, *splish-splash*, what! Water rose in the hole.

"Eh, eh!" cried Frog. "What's happening?"

Slish-slosh, the water rose higher and higher, and Frog was flooded out of his home. He waved to Hen as he floated by her hut, and sang:

"All in together now

How do you like the weather now?"

"Sing it!" said Hen. "But you'll soon croon another tune."

It wasn't long before the steady force of the rain stung Frog's tender skin, and he began to wail:

"Kwo kwa kwee

Kwa kwee kwo

The stinging rain is riddling me

Where shall I go?"

Frog knew where he planned to go. He bounded for shelter. Hop, hop, hop, hop, hop, hop right up to Hen's hut.

"Hen, Hen!" he cried as he rapped on her door. "May I come into your hut?"

"No," said Hen. "Uh-uh! When I asked you to help me make a hut, you refused."

"If you don't let me come in," said Frog, "I'll call Cat, the cat that eats little chickens."

"Go back to your hole!" said Hen.

"Cat! Cat!" yelled Frog. "Come and eat Hen."

"Shh," said Hen. She opened the door. "Hush your mouth! Shame on you, scamp! Come on in."

Frog hopped in and sat by the door. The rain beat down, but Hen's hut was tight and the rain couldn't get in. Frog leaned against the door drumming his numb toes and rubbing his stinging skin. Hen sat by the fire.

"Hen," said Frog, "may I warm myself by the fire?"

"No," said Hen. "Uh-uh!

You didn't help me make the hut,
  Hands on your hips.
You didn't help me gather wood,
  Pursed your lips."

"If you don't let me sit by the fire," said Frog, "I'll call Cat, the cat that eats little chickens."

"That's not fair, Frog, you wouldn't dare."

Frog opened the door and cried:

"Cat! Cat! Here's Hen Chick
  Come and eat her! Quick, come quick!"

Hen slammed and bolted the door.

"Scamp!" she said. "You scim-scam-scamp! Go ahead then, sit by the fire."

Frog hopped beside Hen and warmed himself by the fire.

"Umm-umm," he said, "fire sure feels good."

Frog spread his tingling toes to the heat and stroked his skin. Hen busied herself roasting corn. Then she began to eat.

"Hen," said Frog, "may I have some corn?"

"No," said Hen. "Uh-uh!
  You didn't help me make the hut,
  Hands on your hips.
  You didn't help me gather wood,
  Pursed your lips.
  You didn't help me pick the corn,
  Rolled your eyes."

"Ah! so what," said Frog. "If you don't give me some corn to eat, then I'll call Cat, the cat that eats little chickens."

"And I'll call your bluff," said Hen.

Frog opened the window and called:

"Cat! Cat! Here's Hen Chick
  Come and eat her! Quick, come quick!"

Hen slammed and latched the window.

"Scamp!" she cried. "Greedy scamp! Here, help yourself."

Frog helped himself until all the corn was eaten. Then he rubbed his stomach, stretched himself and leaned back on his elbow. The food and the fire made Frog drowsy. He yawned.

"Hen," said Frog, "may I lie on your bed?"

"No!" said Hen. "Uh-uh!

You didn't help me make the hut,

Hands on your hips.

You didn't help me gather wood,

Pursed your lips.

You didn't help me pick the corn,

Rolled your eyes.

You didn't help me make the bed,

An' it ain't your size!"

"If you don't let me lie on your bed," said Frog, "I'll call Cat, the cat that eats little chickens."

"Shh, shh!" said Hen.

Frog jumped up and down and bawled:

"Cat! Cat! Here's Hen Chick

Come and eat her! Quick, come quick!"

"Quiet, scamp!" said Hen. "Lazy scamp! Go ahead then, lie on my bed."

Frog lay on Hen's bed and fell fast asleep. He was still snoring loudly when the rain stopped.

Hen stepped outdoors to see if the pumpkins were still on the roof. She kept an eye cocked for Cat.

"Well, all right!" she said. "Just where I left them."

She went in and slammed the door, *bligh!*

Frog sprang awake. The noise frightened him, and he dived under the bed.

"Come on out, Frog," said Hen. "The storm's over."

Frog crawled out.

"I'm hungry," he said.

30

"Climb onto the roof and fetch us some pumpkins," said Hen. "I'll cook, and we'll eat."

"Umm," said Frog. "Umm, pumpkin. I love pumpkin." But he still just sat on the edge of the bed.

Hen looked out of the window. She saw a small dark cloud in the distance. She knew that sign well, uh-huh!

"Hop to it, Frog," she said. "You can rest while I'm cooking a pumpkin."

Frog went outside and climbed up onto the roof. He dislodged a pumpkin from the thatch and rolled it down. Hen stood by the window and watched the dark cloud approach. It came faster and faster and grew bigger and bigger and . . .

It was Hawk!

Hawk spied Frog rolling the pumpkins off the roof. Frog was too busy to notice anything, not even Hawk's shadow as Hawk hovered over the thatch.

Hawk closed his wings and fell swiftly, silently. Suddenly, *flump!* Hawk snatched Frog in his claws and took off.

"Help! Help!" cried Frog. "Hen, help me, help! I'm being carried off."

"Eh, eh!" said Hen. "Why don't you call Cat? You know, the Cat that eats little chickens. Eh? Click, clack, cluck, claa, clee."

Hen watched the scene safely from her window. Hawk soared upwards.

"Good!" said Hen. "That's it. Take the little so-and-so away. I've had more than enough of him, little tough buttocks!"

Hawk flew higher and higher. If Frog did call Cat, Cat did not come.

So that was that. Hawk took Frog away, and Hen could relax again. She cooked the pumpkin and sat down to eat. She was so happy that she ate eighteen plates of pumpkin without a stop. Then she lay back on her little bed and sang:

"Click clack cluck
Click claa clee.
I ate pumpkin,
Pumpkin didn't eat me."

31

La Hormiguita
(The Little Ant)

a tale from Spanish New Mexico
retold by Joe Hayes

All through the long, cold winter La Hormiguita, the little ant, had to stay inside her underground home because the ground was all covered with snow. But now the snow was melted, so she went to the door with her mother to see if spring had come.

"Look, Mamá," she said, "the snow has melted. And the grass is turning green. It's springtime! May I go outside and play?"

"No, *Mi 'jita,*" her mother said. "Don't you see those dark clouds? And can't you feel how cold it is? It may still snow. You'd better stay inside."

But La Hormiguita didn't do as she was told. When her mother was busy, she ran outside to play. She climbed to the very tip of each green blade of grass she came to. She ran upside down on low branches of bushes and trees. She went a long way from home.

But pretty soon La Hormiguita began to feel cold. "Mamá was right," she thought. "I'm going back inside."

But just as she started for home, big, papery flakes of snow began to float down from the sky. And one big snowflake landed right on La Hormiguita's little leg and stuck it fast to the ground.

La Hormiguita tugged and tugged at her little leg. And she cried out to *La Nieve,* the snow, to let go of it so she could go home. She said:

| *Nieve, suelta mi patita* | Snow, let go of my leg |
| *pá que vaya a mi casita!* | so that I can go home! |

But the snow wouldn't let go of her little leg. So La
Hormiguita called out to *El Sol*, the sun, to melt the snow:

Sol, derrite Nieve.	Sun, melt the snow.
Nieve, suelta mi patita	Snow, let go of my leg
pá que vaya a mi casita!	so that I can go home!

But the sun wouldn't melt the snow. So La Hormiguita called
out to *La Nube*, the cloud, to cover the sun:

Nube, tapa Sol.	Cloud, cover the sun.
Sol, derrite Nieve.	Sun, melt the snow.
Nieve, suelta mi patita	Snow, let go of my leg
pá que vaya a mi casita!	so that I can go home!

But the cloud wouldn't cover the sun. So La Hormiguita
called out to *El Viento*, the wind, to scatter the cloud:

Viento, desbarata Nube.	Wind, scatter the cloud.
Nube, tapa Sol.	Cloud, cover the sun.
Sol, derrite Nieve.	Sun, melt the snow.
Nieve, suelta mi patita	Snow, let go of my leg
pá que vaya a mi casita!	so that I can go home!

But the wind wouldn't scatter the cloud. So La Hormiguita
called out to *La Pared*, the wall, to block the wind:

Pared, ataja Viento.	Wall, block the wind.
Viento, desbarata Nube.	Wind, scatter the cloud.
Nube, tapa Sol.	Cloud, cover the sun.
Sol, derrite Nieve.	Sun, melt the snow.
Nieve, suelta mi patita	Snow, let go of my leg
pá que vaya a mi casita!	so that I can go home!

But the wall wouldn't block the wind. So La Hormiguita
called out to *El Ratón*, the mouse, to gnaw holes in the wall:

Ratón, agujerea Pared.	Mouse, gnaw holes in the wall.
Pared, ataja Viento.	Wall, block the wind.
Viento, desbarata Nube.	Wind, scatter the cloud.
Nube, tapa Sol.	Cloud, cover the sun.
Sol, derrite Nieve.	Sun, melt the snow.
Nieve, suelta mi patita	Snow, let go of my leg
pá que vaya a mi casita!	so that I can go home!

But the mouse wouldn't gnaw holes in the wall. So La Hormiguita called out to *El Gato*, the cat, to catch the mouse:

Gato, coge Ratón.	Cat, catch the mouse.
Ratón agujerea Pared.	Mouse, gnaw holes in the wall.
Pared, ataja Viento.	Wall, block the wind.
Viento, desbarata Nube.	Wind, scatter the cloud.
Nube, tapa Sol.	Cloud, cover the sun.
Sol, derrite Nieve.	Sun, melt the snow.
Nieve, suelta mi patita	Snow, let go of my leg
pá que vaya a mi casita!	so that I can go home!

But the cat wouldn't catch the mouse. So La Hormiguita called out to *El Perro*, the dog, to chase the cat:

Perro, persigue Gato.	Dog, chase the cat.
Gato, coge Ratón.	Cat, catch the mouse.
Ratón agujerea Pared.	Mouse, gnaw holes in the wall.
Pared, ataja Viento.	Wall, block the wind.
Viento, desbarata Nube.	Wind, scatter the cloud.
Nube, tapa Sol.	Cloud, cover the sun.
Sol, derrite Nieve.	Sun, melt the snow.
Nieve, suelta mi patita	Snow, let go of my leg
pá que vaya a mi casita!	So that I can go home!

But do you think the dog would chase the cat? No! He wouldn't do it. So La Hormiguita called out to *La Pulga*, the little flea that lives on the dog, to bite the dog:

Pulga, pica Perro.	Flea, bite the dog.
Perro, persigue Gato.	Dog, chase the cat.
Gato, coge Ratón.	Cat, catch the mouse.
Ratón, agujerea Pared.	Mouse, gnaw holes in the wall.
Pared, ataja Viento.	Wall, block the wind.
Viento, desbarata Nube.	Wind, scatter the cloud.
Nube, tapa Sol.	Cloud, cover the sun.
Sol, derrite Nieve.	Sun, melt the snow.
NIEVE, SUELTA MI PATITA	SNOW, LET GO OF MY LEG
PÁ QUE VAYA A MI CASITA!	SO THAT I CAN GO HOME!

Well! The flea is a cousin to the ant. And when she heard La Hormiguita crying out for help:

> The flea began to bite the dog.
> The dog began to chase the cat.
> The cat began to catch the mouse.
> The mouse began to gnaw the wall.
> The wall began to block the wind.
> The wind began to scatter the cloud.
> The cloud began to block the sun.
> The sun began to melt the snow . . .

The snow let go of La Hormiguita's little leg. And she finally made it back home safely.

And she waited until her mother said that *spring had come for sure* before she went back outside to play.

The OWL and the PUSSY-CAT

a poem by
Edward Lear

The Owl and the Pussy-Cat went to sea
   In a beautiful pea-green boat:
They took some honey, and plenty of money
   Wrapped up in a five-pound note.
The Owl looked up to the stars above,
   And sang to a small guitar,
"O lovely Pussy, O Pussy, my love,
   What a beautiful Pussy you are,
      You are,
      You are!
   What a beautiful Pussy you are!"

Pussy said to the Owl, "You elegant fowl,
   How charmingly sweet you sing!
Oh! let us be married; too long we have tarried:
   But what shall we do for a ring?"
They sailed away, for a year and a day,
   To the land where the bong-tree grows;
And there in a wood a Piggy-wig stood,
   With a ring at the end of his nose.
      His nose,
      His nose,
   With a ring at the end of his nose.

"Dear Pig, are you willing to sell for one shilling
   Your ring?" Said the Piggy, "I will."
So they took it away, and were married next day
   By the Turkey who lives on the hill.
They dined on mince and slices of quince,
   Which they ate with a runcible spoon;
And hand in hand, on the edge of the sand
   They danced by the light of the moon,
      The moon,
      The moon,
   They danced by the light of the moon.

How Our People Came to Be

*a legend told by Arizona Indian children
to Byrd Baylor*

In the first days of the world there were no people. The maker of the world wanted people walking around the desert and he wanted them to be a beautiful brown color so he made them out of sand and water.

Out of little bits of mud he shaped the first people. They were the Cocopah and Maricopa and Quechan Indians. He told them they could have the desert to live in and he showed them everything they would need to know to get along in a hot dry place. He taught them what plants to eat and what ceremonies to do to make rain come.

This maker of the world was called KWIKUMAT. He had special colors of his own—red and black. He told the people to remember that red was for blood because blood gives life and that black was for the darkness that means death.

To thank him for making us, we use those same colors now in the special clothes we wear for ceremonies. And we keep this design of KWIKUMAT in our tribe. It is supposed to remind us of how we started and it also reminds us that life and death are part of every person. They go together.

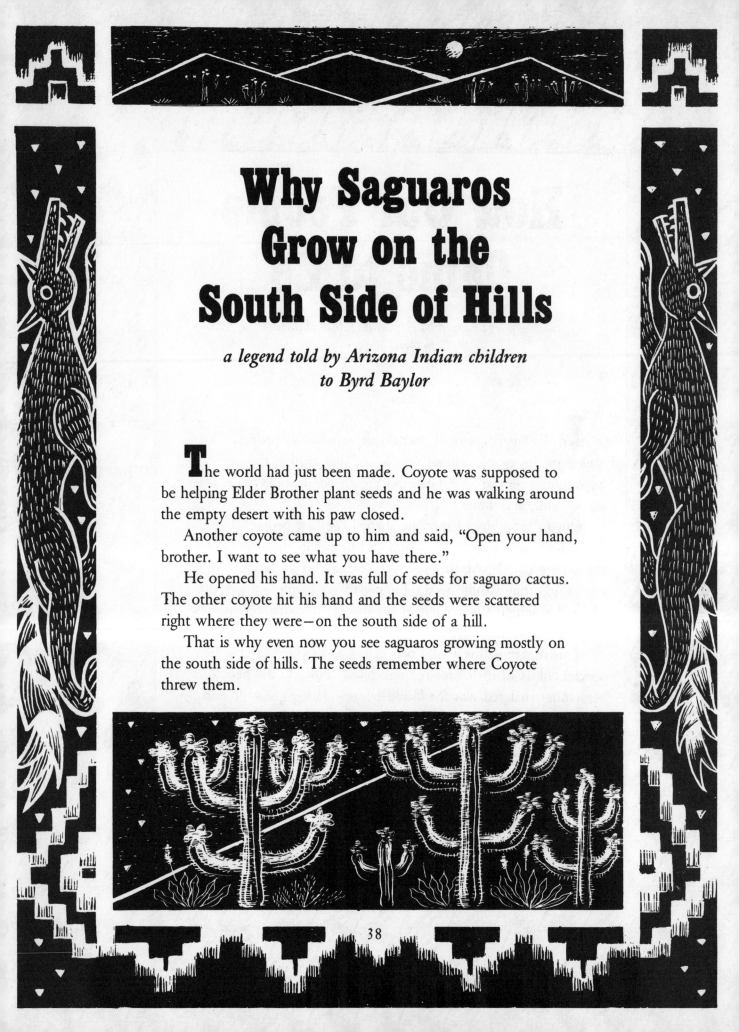

Why Saguaros Grow on the South Side of Hills

*a legend told by Arizona Indian children
to Byrd Baylor*

The world had just been made. Coyote was supposed to
be helping Elder Brother plant seeds and he was walking around
the empty desert with his paw closed.

Another coyote came up to him and said, "Open your hand,
brother. I want to see what you have there."

He opened his hand. It was full of seeds for saguaro cactus.
The other coyote hit his hand and the seeds were scattered
right where they were—on the south side of a hill.

That is why even now you see saguaros growing mostly on
the south side of hills. The seeds remember where Coyote
threw them.

Turkey Makes the Corn and Coyote Plants It

a White Mountain Apache tale
retold by Richard Erdoes and Alfonso Ortiz

Long ago when all the animals talked like people, Turkey overheard a boy begging his sister for food. "What does your little brother want?" he asked the girl. "He's hungry, but we have nothing to eat," she said.

When Turkey heard this, he shook himself all over. Many kinds of fruits and wild food dropped out of his body, and the brother and sister ate these up. Turkey shook himself again, and a variety of corn that is very large dropped out of his feathers. He shook himself a third time, and yellow corn dropped out. And when he shook himself for the fourth time, white corn dropped out.

Bear came over, and Turkey told him, "I'm helping to feed my sister and my brother, over there." Bear said, "You can shake only four times to make food come out of you, but I have every kind of food on me, from my feet to my head."

Bear shook himself, and out of his fur dropped juniper berries. He shook himself again, and out dropped a cactus that is good to eat. Then he shook out acorns, then another kind of cactus, then Gambel oak acorns, then blue oak acorns, then piñon nuts, then a species of sumac, then manzanita berries, then wild mulberries, then *saguaro* fruit.

Turkey said to the boy and girl, "I have four kinds of corn seeds here for you, and this is a good place to plant them." The sister and

39

brother cut digging sticks and made holes with them. In the holes they planted all their corn seeds. The next day the corn had already come up and was about a foot and a half high. The girl said, "We still have some squash seeds here," so they planted them too.

The boy and girl asked Turkey for more corn seed. "The corn is coming up nicely," they said, "so we want to make another farm and plant more corn there." Turkey gave them the seed, and they left him to look after their first fields while they started off to make the other farm.

 When they came back, they heard Turkey hollering at the corn field. They ran down there and saw him dragging one wing along the ground on the side toward them. There were snakes on the other side of him, and he pretended to have a broken wing to lure the snakes away and shield the boy and girl. The squash plants had young squash on them, and the corn had grown tall and formed ears and tassels. The tassels had pollen in them, and the snakes had come to gather the pollen out of the corn plants. Turkey told the boy and girl to stay away from the corn for four days, when the snakes would be finished. At the end of the four days, the corn was ripe. Turkey told them, "This will be the only time when the corn will come up in four days. From now on it will take quite a while." And it does.

By now the brother and sister had planted corn three times, and they gave seeds to other people. Then Slim Coyote came and asked for some. "The corn you planted is growing well, and the ears are coming out on it," he said. "I'd like to have some seeds to plant for myself."

Coyote would have to do lots of work if he wanted to raise his corn, but that wasn't his plan. "These other people here plant their corn, and after it's grown, they have to cook it. Me, I'm not going to do it that way. I'll cook my corn first and then plant it, so I won't have to bother to cook it when it's ripe." Here's where Coyote made a big mistake. He cooked his corn, ate some, and planted quite a patch of the rest. He felt pretty good about it. "Now I've done well for myself. You people have to cook your corn after you plant it, but mine will be already cooked," he said.

After planting, he went off with the rest of the people to gather acorns, but when they returned to their fields, Coyote's had nothing growing on it at all. He said angrily, "You people must have taken the hearts out of the corn seeds you gave to me." "No, we didn't do that," they told him, "but you cooked the heart out of them before you planted."

Coyote asked for more seeds and planted them the right way this time. So his corn grew: the day after he planted, it was up about a foot and a half. He felt good.

The people who had planted their corn at the beginning were harvesting now and tying it up into bundles. Coyote saw these and wanted some. People got mad at Coyote because he was always asking them for corn. "I just want some green ears to feed my children," he would say. "As soon as my corn is ripe, I'll pay you back."

The other people had all their corn in and stripped now, but their squashes were still growing in the field. Coyote stole their squash, and the people all came to his camp. They wanted to know if he was the one who was stealing their squash. Coyote pretended to get angry. "You're always blaming me for stealing everything. There are lots of camps over there. Why do you have to choose mine to come to with your accusations?" But the people knew about Coyote's thieving ways.

"From now on, don't make your farm near us. Move away and live someplace else!" they said.

"All right. There are several of you that I was going to repay with corn, but I won't do it now that you've treated me this way," he said. So Coyote's family lived poorly, and they never bothered to cook anything before they ate it.

KANJI-JO, THE NESTLINGS

a Mende folk tale from West Africa retold
by Margaret Read MacDonald

On the banks of the Kanji River
a mother bird laid five eggs.
For a long time she sat on those eggs.
She fluffed her feathers over them and kept them warm.

Now and then she would sing to the eggs.
   "I laid five eggs long ago . . .
   By the Kanji River-o . . .
   I laid five eggs long ago . . . ."

Then she would stand and fluff her feathers.
   "Kanji-jo, gebeti-jo.
   Kanji-jo, gebeti-jo.
   Kanji-jo, gebeti-jo."

Just when the chicks were about to pop from their eggs a hunter
came by.
He threw a net over the mother bird and carried her off.
After a while, she managed to escape,
but by that time she was far from her nest.

Meanwhile, the sun shone so warmly on the eggs
that they began to hatch.
The first egg rolled over
    "peck . . . peck . . . peck . . ."
Out came a baby bird.

The second egg began to move.
    "peck . . . peck . . . peck . . ."
Out popped another.

The third egg . . .
    "peck . . . peck . . . peck . . ."

The fourth . . .
    "peck . . . peck . . . peck . . ."

The fifth egg . . .
    "peck . . . peck . . . peck . . .
    peck . . . peck . . . peck . . .
    peck . . . peck . . . PECK!"

There were five baby birds in the nest.

    "Ma-má! Ma-má! Ma-má!"
They began at once to cry for their mother.

    "Ma-má! Ma-má! Ma-má!"
But there was no mother there for the chicks.

    "Our mother has gone!
    We must look for our mother!"

The little birds climbed down out of their nest.
They began wobbling down the road on their weak little legs.

"Ma-má! Ma-má! Ma-má!"

They met Mrs. Bushfowl.
"Ma-má! Ma-má! Ma-má!"
"Oh dear, are these MY children?" said Mrs. Bushfowl.
"I didn't know I had five children.
But they are calling me 'Ma-má.'
They must be mine."
She took the little chicks into her nest.
She fed them their supper.
She put them to bed for the night.

In the morning the five little birds looked at their new mother.
She was big and brown and fluffy.
They were small and their feathers seemed to be blue.

"Pardon us, but are you really our mother?
Our mother sang a beautiful song when we were in our eggs.
Would you sing your song, so we will know you are our
      mother?"

Mrs. Bushfowl fluffed up her feathers.
She began to sing.
"ko-ko-ye! ko-ko-ye! ko-ko-ye!
ko-ko-ye! ko-ko-ye! ko-ko-ye!"

"THAT'S not our mother's song.
Our mother sang a beautiful song.
She sang like this:

"I laid five eggs long ago . . .
By the Kanji River-o . . .
I laid five eggs long ago. . . .

44

Kanji-jo, gebeti-jo.
Kanji-jo, gebeti-jo.
Kanji-jo, gebeti-jo."

"That's a lovely song," said Mrs. Bushfowl.
"But I can't sing like that.
I must not be your mother.
You'd better go look for her."

So the little birds went on down the road.
They were feeling stronger now.
They marched along calling:

"Ma-má! Ma-má! Ma-má!"

In the evening they met Mrs. Dove.
"Ma-má! Ma-má! Ma-má!"
"Oh my, are these MY children?" said Mrs. Dove.
"I didn't know I had five children.
But they are calling me 'Ma-má!'
They must be mine."

She took them into her nest.
She fed them their supper.
She put them to bed for the night.

In the morning the five little chicks looked at their new mother.
She was shaped in a special dove way.
She seemed not like them at all.

"Pardon us, but are you really our mother?
Our mother sang a beautiful song when we were in our eggs.
Would you sing your song, so we will know you are our
        mother?"

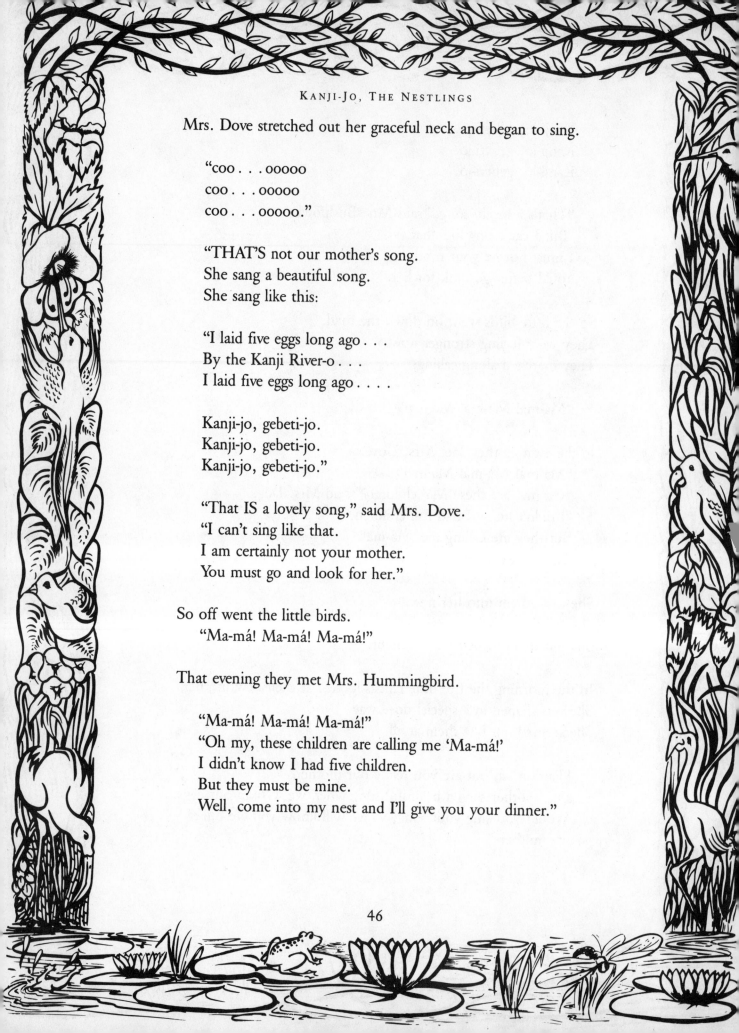

Mrs. Dove stretched out her graceful neck and began to sing.

"coo . . . ooooo
coo . . . ooooo
coo . . . ooooo."

"THAT'S not our mother's song.
She sang a beautiful song.
She sang like this:

"I laid five eggs long ago . . .
By the Kanji River-o . . .
I laid five eggs long ago . . . .

Kanji-jo, gebeti-jo.
Kanji-jo, gebeti-jo.
Kanji-jo, gebeti-jo."

"That IS a lovely song," said Mrs. Dove.
"I can't sing like that.
I am certainly not your mother.
You must go and look for her."

So off went the little birds.
"Ma-má! Ma-má! Ma-má!"

That evening they met Mrs. Hummingbird.

"Ma-má! Ma-má! Ma-má!"
"Oh my, these children are calling me 'Ma-má!'
I didn't know I had five children.
But they must be mine.
Well, come into my nest and I'll give you your dinner."

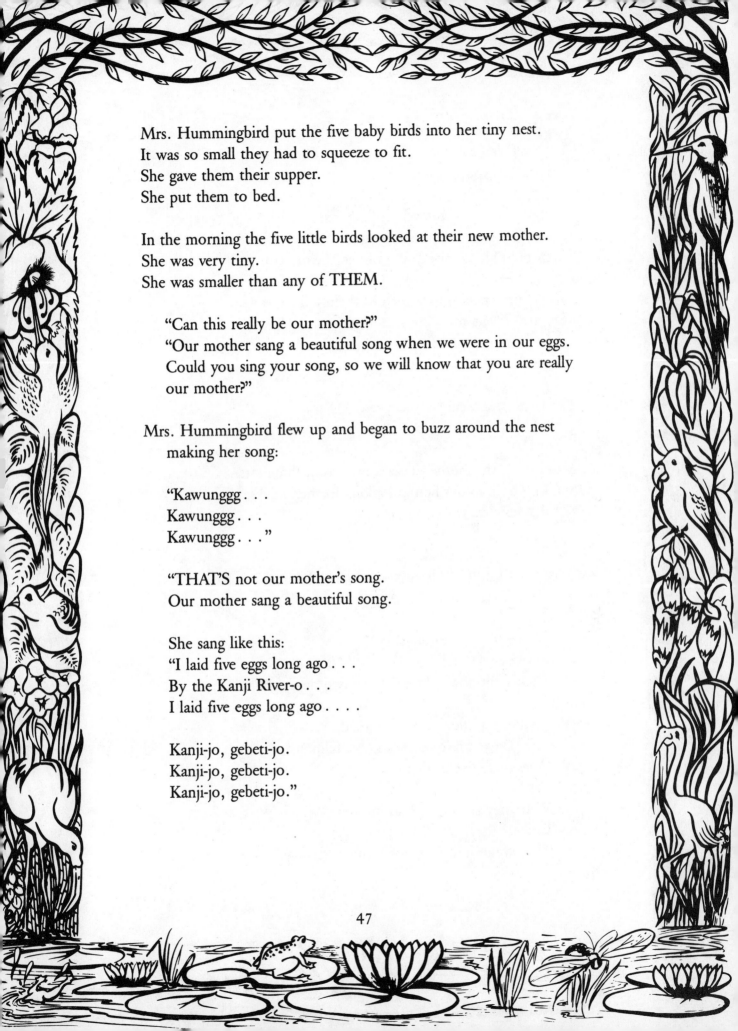

Mrs. Hummingbird put the five baby birds into her tiny nest.
It was so small they had to squeeze to fit.
She gave them their supper.
She put them to bed.

In the morning the five little birds looked at their new mother.
She was very tiny.
She was smaller than any of THEM.

"Can this really be our mother?"
"Our mother sang a beautiful song when we were in our eggs.
Could you sing your song, so we will know that you are really
our mother?"

Mrs. Hummingbird flew up and began to buzz around the nest
making her song:

"Kawunggg . . .
Kawunggg . . .
Kawunggg . . ."

"THAT'S not our mother's song.
Our mother sang a beautiful song.

She sang like this:
"I laid five eggs long ago . . .
By the Kanji River-o . . .
I laid five eggs long ago . . . .

Kanji-jo, gebeti-jo.
Kanji-jo, gebeti-jo.
Kanji-jo, gebeti-jo."

"What a lovely song!
I can't sing like that.
I am not your mother.

"But you are such lovely little birds
and you sing such a fine song
I would like to give you a present before you go."

Mrs. Hummingbird gave each of them a little present.
  "Here is one for you . . . and you . . . and you . . . and
      you . . . and you.
I hope you find your mother."

The little birds went on their way.
  "Ma-má! Ma-má! Ma-má!"

Meanwhile, the mother had escaped from the hunter.
She flew back to her home, looking for her chicks.
But the nest was empty.

She flew down the road.
  "Mrs. Bushfowl! Have you seen my children?"
  "Were there five of them?"
  "Yes."
  "Did they sing a lovely song?"
  "I expect they did."
  "They went down the road just two days ago."

The mother bird flew down the road.
  "Mrs. Dove! Have you seen my children?"
  "Were there five of them?"
  "Yes."
  "Were they singing a beautiful song?"
  "I expect they were."
  "They went down this road, just yesterday."

The mother bird flew down the road.
    "Mrs. Hummingbird! Have you seen my children?"
    "Were there five of them?"
    "Yes."
    "Did they have blue feathers like yours?"
    "I believe they should have."
    "Were they singing a fine song?"

    "I believe they were."
    "Then they were just here.
    They went down this road."

"Aaaahhhhh. . . ."
The mother bird ran after her children.
"Chick . . . chick . . . chick . . . chick . . ."
"Ma-má! Ma-má! Ma-má!"
Then the chicks heard her.
They turned and looked at their mother.
Her feathers were blue like theirs, only more brilliant.
She was shaped just like they were, only bigger.
She was just the right size to be their mother.
The five little chicks RAN to their mother.
    "MA-MA! MA-MA! MA-MA! MA-MA! MA-MA!"
    "CHICK! CHICK! CHICK! CHICK! CHICK!"
They hugged one another.
They ruffled one another's feathers.

The mother bird made a nest for her babies.
She fed them.
She put them to bed for the night.

    "Sing us your song!
    Sing us your song!
    So we will know you are really our mother!"

"Wait," said the mother bird.
"In the morning we will sing.
In the morning we will dance.
In the morning I will teach you how to fly."

In the morning the mother bird woke up first of all.
She stretched her head way over the nest and looked at her
    sleeping children.
And she began to sing.

    "I laid five eggs long ago . . .
     By the Kanji River-o . . .
     I laid five eggs long ago. . . ."
When the little birds heard that
they jumped to their feet and began to flap their wings and dance!
    "Kanji-jo, gebeti-jo!
    Kanji-jo, gebeti-jo!
    Kanji-jo, gebeti-jo!"

It really was their mother.

And all day long they danced in that nest.
    "Kanji-jo, gebeti-jo . . .
    Kanji-jo, gebeti-jo . . .
    Kanji-jo, gebeti-jo. . . ."

The Emperor's New Clothes

a Danish fairy tale by Hans Christian Andersen
adapted by Amy Ehrlich

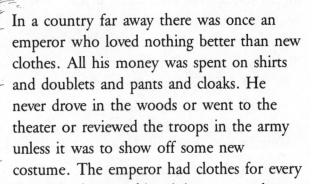

In a country far away there was once an emperor who loved nothing better than new clothes. All his money was spent on shirts and doublets and pants and cloaks. He never drove in the woods or went to the theater or reviewed the troops in the army unless it was to show off some new costume. The emperor had clothes for every hour of the day and evening, and whenever his ministers wanted to find him, they had only to look in his dressing room.

Life was very gay in the great town where he lived. The streets were thronged with strangers, and one day two swindlers were among them. They made themselves out to be weavers and said they could weave cloth more beautiful than any on earth. Not only were the colors and patterns superb, but the garments that were made from the cloth had the amazing quality of becoming invisible to all who were dull and incompetent. Or so the swindlers claimed.

"Those must be wonderful clothes," thought the emperor when he heard the story. "By wearing them I shall be able to tell wise men from fools and learn who among my people deserves my trust. Yes, I must have some of that cloth woven for me at once." And he gave the two swindlers large sums of money so they could begin work.

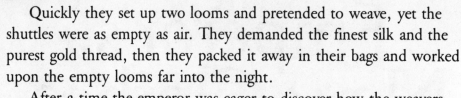

Quickly they set up two looms and pretended to weave, yet the shuttles were as empty as air. They demanded the finest silk and the purest gold thread, then they packed it away in their bags and worked upon the empty looms far into the night.

After a time the emperor was eager to discover how the weavers were getting on with the cloth. But remembering that anyone who was a fool would not be able to see it, he became reluctant to go into the room himself. "Of course I have no fears about my own competence," he thought. "But still it may be best to send some other man. My oldest minister is the one for the task. He is clever and will be able to judge the quality of the cloth at once."

And so the old minister went to find the weavers. There they sat before their empty looms, working the invisible thread as though it were real. "How can this be?" thought the man, opening his eyes very wide. "I see nothing, nothing at all."

The swindlers stood up then and asked him how he liked the unusual design and the beautiful colors. They pointed to the empty looms and the minister stared as hard as he could, but he could see nothing, for there was nothing. "Could it mean that I am stupid?" he thought fearfully. "I have never thought so, but who can be certain? Nobody must be allowed to know that I cannot see the cloth."

"Well, what do you think of it?" asked one of the weavers.

"Oh, it is beautiful. Most exquisite. I shall certainly tell the emperor how pleased I am," said the minister.

Then the weavers drew him closer to the empty looms. They named the different colors and described the pattern, and the minister listened closely so that he could repeat it all to the emperor.

Now the weavers demanded more money and more silk for their work, but again they put it into their own pockets and went on weaving at the empty looms.

A short time later the emperor sent another minister to learn how the cloth was getting on and if it would soon be ready. The man looked and looked but he could see only the empty looms. He blinked once and then again and still he saw nothing. "I know I am not a fool," he thought. "So it must mean I am unfit for my position. I must never let on that I cannot see the cloth." And he went back to the emperor and praised the beautiful colors and the design he had never seen. Soon everyone in the town was talking about the splendid cloth.

As last the emperor could wait no longer and decided to see it for himself. Accompanied by a large number of servants and his two faithful ministers, he went into the room where the weavers were working. They moved their hands fast across the looms, yet there was not a strand of silk upon them.

"Is the cloth not magnificent, Your Majesty?" asked the two ministers. "Surely you will agree with all our praise of it." And they pointed to the empty looms, for each thought the others could see the cloth.

The emperor was struck with horror. "What!" he thought. "I see nothing! This is terrible. Am I a fool? Am I unfit to be emperor?" But knowing that the others were awaiting his response, he nodded and smiled and clapped his hands together. "Perfectly wonderful! Superb!" he said, gazing at the empty loom.

"Perfectly wonderful! Superb!" the servants echoed, though they saw no more than the others.

The very next day there was to be a great procession, and everyone agreed that the emperor must lead it dressed in garments sewn from the wonderful cloth. Then the emperor gave each of the weavers a decoration for his buttonhole and the title of Knight of the Loom.

The night before the procession the weavers sat up until dawn, burning sixteen candles so that people would see how hard they were working to get the emperor's new clothes ready. They pretended to take the cloth off the loom. Then they cut it out in the air with a huge pair of shears and stitched it together using needles without any thread. "Now the emperor's new clothes are ready," they announced.

When the emperor went into the room with his ministers and servants, both of the weavers raised one arm in the air as if they were holding something very precious. "These are the pants; this is the coat; here is the mantle," they said. "As you can see, the cloth is as light and delicate as a spider's web. One might almost think one had nothing on, but that is the very beauty of it."

"Yes, oh yes!" everyone cried, staring harder than ever at nothing.

"Please, Your Majesty, you must take off your clothes so we may put the new ones on here before the mirror," the weavers said.

"Of course. Quite so," said the emperor and he took off all his clothes. Then the weavers pretended to fasten something around his waist and tie something else around his neck, and finally they ran their hands along the floor as if they were arranging the train.

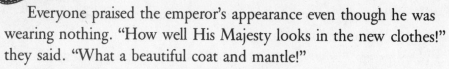

Everyone praised the emperor's appearance even though he was wearing nothing. "How well His Majesty looks in the new clothes!" they said. "What a beautiful coat and mantle!"

"The canopy that will be held over Your Majesty is here. The procession is about to begin!" the oldest minister cried.

The emperor turned round and round in front of the mirror as if admiring his reflection. "Very well, I am ready," he announced. He walked with dignity from the weavers' room, and the chamberlains who were to carry the train pretended to lift it from the ground and hold it with their hands in the air.

Then the emperor walked at the head of the procession under the beautiful canopy, and everyone in the streets cried, "Look at the emperor's new clothes. Are they not the most wonderful he has ever worn?" They did not dare admit they could see nothing for fear they would be called fools. Never before had the emperor's clothes been so much admired.

"But he has got nothing on," said a little child.

"Oh, listen to the innocent," said the father. And one person whispered to another what the child had said. "He has nothing on. A child says he has nothing on!"

"But he has nothing on!" all the people cried at last.

The emperor felt a shudder go through him, for he knew at once that it was true, but he had to continue to lead the procession. And so he walked on beneath the canopy, and the chamberlains held up the invisible train.

Little
Red Riding Hood

a German folk tale
retold by Margaret H. Lippert

Once upon a time there was a little girl who was so kind that everyone loved her. Her grandmother had made her a little red cloak with a hood. The girl liked it so much that she wore it all the time, so everyone called her Little Red Riding Hood.

One day her mother said to her, "Here is a basket of bread and cheese for you to take to Grandmother. She is not feeling well, and the food will be good for her. Walk quickly and stay on the path."

"I will, Mother," said Little Red Riding Hood.

Her grandmother lived in the woods not too far from the village. When Little Red Riding Hood got to the woods, she met a wolf. She was not afraid of him because she did not know how wicked he was.

"Good morning," said the wolf. "Where are you going?"

"I am taking some bread and cheese to my grandmother."

"Where does she live?" asked the wolf.

"Her house is on this path under three big oak trees," said Little Red Riding Hood.

55

The wolf thought, "She would be a delicious morsel. But if I am clever, I think I can snap up the old woman, too."

They went along together for a while. Then the wolf said, "Look at all the pretty wildflowers. Perhaps your grandmother would like some."

Little Red Riding Hood looked down at the bright flowers. "I'm sure Grandmother would like a bunch of flowers," she thought. So she picked one, and then another, wandering farther and farther from the path.

While Little Red Riding Hood was picking flowers, the wolf ran to Grandmother's house.

The wolf knocked on the door of the cottage.

"Who is there?" called Grandmother.

"Little Red Riding Hood," said the wolf. "I've brought you some bread and cheese. Please open the door!"

"I am too weak to get up," called the woman. "Lift the latch."

The wolf lifted the latch and the door flew open. He jumped onto the bed and ate up the poor old woman. Then he put on her nightgown and nightcap, got into bed, and pulled up the covers.

Little Red Riding Hood picked flowers until she could carry no more. Then she went on to her grandmother's house. When she got there, she was surprised to see that the door stood open. She was afraid, but she did not know why.

"Good morning, Grandmother," she called. There was no answer. She went up to the bed. There lay her grandmother, with her cap pulled down over her face. She looked very strange.

"Oh Grandmother, what big ears you have," said Little Red Riding Hood.

"The better to hear you with, my dear."

"Grandmother, what big eyes you have."

"The better to see you with, my dear."

"But Grandmother, what big teeth you have."

"The better to eat you with," said the wolf.

At that, he jumped out of bed and swallowed poor Little Red Riding Hood. Then he went back to bed and was soon snoring loudly.

A hunter went past the house and thought, "How loudly the old lady is snoring. I must see if there is anything the matter with her." He went in and saw the wolf lying on the old woman's bed.

He was about to shoot the wolf. Suddenly he thought that perhaps the wolf had swallowed the old lady whole. "Maybe I can save her," he thought. So he cut the wolf open with his knife. Out jumped Little Red Riding Hood, followed by her grandmother.

The hunter skinned the wolf and took the skin home. The grandmother ate the bread and cheese, and soon felt strong again.

Little Red Riding Hood thought to herself, "I will never again wander off the path into the forest. From now on I will listen to my mother."

The Wonderful Knapsack

a Danish folk tale
retold by Mary C. Hatch

Once upon a time there was a soldier who had served his king well for ten years and a day, but alas, alack! When he came to get his pay for all the wars he had won, the king was as poor as he, and there were only three pennies left in the royal treasury.

"Well," said the soldier, "I'll not worry about it. I'll take my pay in honor and glory."

"To be sure," said the king, "honor and glory are all very well, but they'll not keep the wolf from the door. I will give you the palace plates. They are pure gold and will sell for a high price."

"Then you could not eat like a king," said the soldier, "and that would never do. No, indeed, Your Majesty! Give me the three pennies and I will be on my way."

"Very well, then," said the king, and he scooped up the three lone pennies from the bottom of the royal treasury and laid them in the hand of the soldier. "May they bring you luck," he said, and the soldier thanked him and went whistling on his way.

Now, when he had walked a mile or so, whom should he meet but an old, old woman, bent in the middle and with scarcely a tooth in her head!

"A penny from the young for the old," begged the old woman.

"A penny!" exclaimed the soldier. "Why, I've but three pennies in the whole, wide world. Still, it matters little if there are three or two," and so he gave the old woman one of the pennies.

Then he walked on another mile or so, till what should he come upon but a second old, old woman more bent and toothless than the first!

"A penny from the young for the old," begged the old woman.

"A penny!" cried the soldier. "Why, all I have in the whole, wide world is two pennies. Still, it matters little if there are two or one," and he gave the old woman the second of the pennies.

Then he walked on with the one lone penny, till after a mile or so he was stopped by a third old, old woman, so bent that her chin almost touched her knees.

"A penny from the young for the old," said the old creature; and the soldier exclaimed, "One penny is all I have in the world! But it matters little if I've one or none," and he gave the last penny to the old woman.

At this, the old creature changed into a young and beautiful girl; for she was not really a withered old woman at all, but a fairy who had tested the soldier three times to see if he were good and brave.

"What a kind and generous lad you are!" exclaimed the fairy. "And for that, you deserve to be generously rewarded. I will give you three wishes, and all of them will come true."

But what do you know, the soldier could not think of a thing to wish for! He had two strong arms, two long legs, and a head set straight on his shoulders, and that was all he had ever wanted. At length, however, he said, "I wish to have a long life and a healthy one."

"You have wished a good wish," said the fairy. "Now for your other wishes."

Now the soldier had a knapsack that had been with him in the wars, and he liked the fit and the feel of it, particularly when it was full; so at last he said, "I wish that my knapsack will never wear out. And I wish last, that whatever I want will go into my knapsack, and whatever I want will come out."

"Three better wishes were never made," said the fairy, "nor three more easily granted. Now good-by, and good luck." And with that the fairy disappeared, and the soldier went happily on his way.

Toward evening he reached the town, and as he was very hungry, in he walked to the best inn and sat down at the finest table. "Landlord," he called, "serve me food, and serve it well," and the landlord came running.

But when the landlord saw a torn and tattered soldier instead of a silk and satin lord, he cried, "We will feed you food aplenty, good soldier, but you must come into the kitchen."

"No, thank you," said the soldier. "This will do quite nicely, I am sure. Of course, I am used to finer linen and brighter candlelight, but as I am hungry, it will not matter. Now bring me a dozen chicken breasts and be quick about it."

At this bold talk, the landlord quickly changed his tune; for of course, no plain, ordinary soldier would speak in such a fashion, and this one must surely be a prince in disguise.

"Yes, sir, whatever you wish, sir," he said politely, and then he ran to set the table with his finest linen and dishes and to serve the food just as the soldier had ordered.

When all was ready, the soldier fell to eating at once, for he was quite famished; but near the end, he remembered to leave a bit on his

plate, since that, of course, is always what lords and ladies do. Then he wished a handful of gold coins into the knapsack, and taking out two of them, tossed them to the landlord.

"I trust this will pay for the meal," he said.

"It is payment, and more," said the landlord, and he bowed so low he bumped his head on the floor. "I hope everything suited your taste, your excellency."

"Fairly well, my good man," said the soldier. "Now you must provide me with a room for the night."

But alas, there were no rooms—and the landlord almost wept to say this—there were no rooms save one, and that could not be used.

"And why not?" exclaimed the soldier.

"Who goes in there alive comes out dead," cried the landlord.

"Is that all?" laughed the soldier. "Then that is the very room for me. Sweep it clean and make the bed well, for I am tired tonight."

The landlord wrung his hands, and the maids cried, and all the rich diners shook their heads; but nothing would do the soldier but to sleep in the dreadful room. So it was prepared; and when the soldier had smoked awhile by the fire and felt a little drowsy, he bade everyone good night and went up to it.

Inside, he locked the door, stood his faithful knapsack in a corner where he could keep his eye on it, and sat down in a chair to see what would happen.

He had only a moment to wait until there was a great rustling in the chimney and a black ball came rolling out of the fireplace and into the center of the room. There it unrolled itself, and the soldier saw the ugliest troll ever seen in the whole, wide world, with eyes red as fire and fingers like claws. Then out rolled a second troll, and after that a third, each uglier than the other, and both much worse than the first.

"How do you do?" said the soldier. "How very nice of you to come and keep me company! Now do sit down and make yourselves at home," and he pointed to three chairs on the other side of the fireplace.

The three trolls seated themselves, but not for long. In a minute they were up and at the soldier. One tweaked his nose, the other pulled his ears, and the third one tried to pin down his arms.

"Dear me!" said the soldier. "I must say this is a strange way for guests to act. Well, if you can do no better, into my knapsack you

must go." And there and then, into the knapsack they had to creep, and soon only a creaking and hissing could be heard.

"I hope you are comfortable there," said the soldier. "But if you are not, 'tis your own fault, to be sure. And now you must answer me a question. Why do you pester this room every night?"

There was a great silence for a moment, but whether they would or nay, the trolls had to give up their secret.

"We guard the oven," said the first.

"To protect a treasure," said the second.

"And woe to him who tries to steal it," said the third.

"Very well," said the soldier, "and thank you for your information." Then he undressed, for he was very tired, and went straight to bed.

Next morning the landlord, and the maids, and all the rich diners came to see what had happened to the remarkable soldier. They knocked on the door and peeked through the keyhole, but as the soldier was still sleeping he did not hear them; so they thought he was dead and set up a great weeping and wailing.

"He was so young and handsome," cried all the maids.

"He was so rich," cried the landlord.

"And he ate like a prince," cried all the rich diners.

Now all this fuss and bother finally awakened the soldier, and he cried out crossly, "Landlord, landlord, what's all this fuss?"

"Oh, my!" cried everyone. "You're not still alive, are you?"

"Alive and ready to eat," answered the soldier. "Landlord, serve me a dozen fresh eggs and a pail of warm milk."

This the landlord ran to do, followed by the maids and diners. When all was ready, the soldier got up and dressed, took a good look at his knapsack, then locked his room and went down to eat.

And when he had eaten, he commanded the landlord to bring him three strong men. "They must take my knapsack to the blacksmith's and beat the dust out of it," said the soldier. "I have walked a long mile or two in my day, and the knapsack is very dusty."

The landlord did as he was ordered, though truth to tell, he considered it quite a strange request. Soon three strong men were lugging and tugging at the knapsack, which looked light as a feather but weighed heavy as lead. When they reached the blacksmith's shop, they were so tired they could hardly lift a finger, to say nothing of wielding a heavy hammer; so three of the blacksmith's strongest helpers were set to the task of beating the knapsack.

But what a shrieking was heard when they started their work, shrieking enough to set your hair on end!

"Don't mind a little noise," said the soldier. "My knapsack is squeaky at the seams. Just beat as hard as you can."

So the men went on, and after a while, all was quiet. Then the soldier said, "There, that's clean enough. Now be so good as to empty it into the sea."

But these poor fellows were now so tired they could scarce lift a finger, to say nothing of carrying a heavy knapsack down to the sea; so three more huskies were found, and they lugged and tugged the strange knapsack down to the shore. Then they opened it, and what a pile of black dust poured into the water! It was all that was left of the three dreadful trolls, and good riddance, too, though it blackened the sea for a mile around.

The workmen were paid for their hard labor, and generously, too, with a handful of gold for each of them; and then the soldier returned to the landlord.

"Landlord," he cried, "I have one last task for you. In the room where I slept last night, there stands a big oven, and this you must tear down at once."

"Well," said the landlord to himself, "he'll soon want to pull down the roof from over my head, but I'll not question money." So he did as the soldier commanded, and there under the oven, what should he find but a pot of gold as big as a washtub!

"What a clever fellow you were to discover all this gold!" exclaimed the landlord.

"Oh, 'twas nothing at all," said the soldier. "Now take it, good landlord, all of it, and use it well." Then he took up his knapsack and bade his host good-by. But the landlord would not let him go without half the money and this he could not refuse. It was a heavy load to carry, so he must stay a bit longer. And then whom should he meet but the landlord's daughter, a very pretty lass, and so he must tarry still longer, till the lass was his bride, and then—well, with health, wealth, and happiness, he no doubt tarries there still.

THE FOX WENT OUT ON A CHILLY NIGHT

an American ballad

The Fox went out on a chilly night,
He prayed for the moon for to give him light,
For he'd many a mile to go that night afore he reached the town-o,
Town-o, town-o,
He'd many a mile to go that night
Afore he reached the town-o.

He ran till he came to a great big bin,
Where the ducks and the geese were put there-in.
"A couple of you will grease my chin afore I leave this town-o,
Town-o, town-o,
A couple of you will grease my chin
Afore I leave this town-o."

He grabbed the gray goose by the neck;
Threw a duck across his back.
He didn't mind their quack, quack, quack
And their legs all dangling down-o.
Down-o, down-o.
He didn't mind their quack, quack, quack
And their legs all dangling down-o.

Then old Mother Flipper-Flopper jumped out of bed.
Out of the window she cocked her head,
Crying, "John, John! The gray goose is gone
And the fox is on the town-o!
Town-o, town-o!"
Crying, "John, John! The gray goose is gone
And the fox is on the town-o!"

Then John he went to the top of the hill;
Blew his horn both loud and shrill;
The fox he said, "I'd better flee with my kill
Or they'll soon be on my trail-o!
Trail-o, trail-o!"
The fox he said, "I'd better flee with my kill
Or they'll soon be on my trail-o!"

He ran till he came to his cozy den,
There were the little ones, eight, nine, ten.
They said, "Daddy, better go back again
'Cause it must be a mighty fine town-o!
Town-o, town-o!"
They said, "Daddy, better go back again
'Cause it must be a mighty fine town-o!"

Then the fox and his wife without any strife,
Cut up the goose with a fork and knife;
They never had such a supper in their life
And the little ones chewed on the bones-o.
Bones-o, bones-o.
They never had such a supper in their life
And the little ones chewed on the bones-o.

The Foolish, Timid Rabbit

a Jataka tale from India
retold by Ellen C. Babbitt

Once upon a time, a Rabbit was asleep under a palm-tree.
All at once he woke up, and thought: "What if the world should
break up! What then would become of me?"

At that moment, some Monkeys dropped a coconut. It fell
down on the ground just back of the Rabbit.

Hearing the noise, the Rabbit said to himself: "The earth is all
breaking up!"

And he jumped up and ran just as fast as he could, without
even looking back to see what made the noise.

Another Rabbit saw him running, and called after him, "What are you running so fast for?"

"Don't ask me!" he cried.

But the other Rabbit ran after him, begging to know what was the matter.

Then the first Rabbit said: "Don't you know? The earth is all breaking up!"

And on he ran, and the second Rabbit ran with him.

The next Rabbit they met ran with them when he heard that the earth was all breaking up.

One Rabbit after another joined them, until there were hundreds of Rabbits running as fast as they could go.

They passed a Deer, calling out to him that the earth was all breaking up. The Deer then ran with them.

The Deer called to a Fox to come along because the earth was all breaking up.

On and on they ran, and an Elephant joined them.

At last the Lion saw the animals running, and heard their cry that the earth was all breaking up.

He thought there must be some mistake, so he ran to the foot of a hill in front of them and roared three times.

This stopped them, for they knew the voice of the King of Beasts, and they feared him.

"Why are you running so fast?" asked the Lion.

"Oh, King Lion," they answered him, "the earth is all breaking up!"

"Who saw it breaking up?" asked the Lion.

"I didn't," said the Elephant. "Ask the Fox—he told me about it."

"I didn't," said the Fox.

"The Rabbits told me about it," said the Deer.

One after another of the Rabbits said: "I did not see it, but another Rabbit told me about it."

At last the Lion came to the Rabbit who had first said the earth was all breaking up.

"Is it true that the earth is all breaking up?" the Lion asked.

"Yes, O Lion, it is," said the Rabbit. "I was asleep under a palm-tree. I woke up and thought, 'What would become of me if the earth should all break up?' At that very moment, I heard the sound of the earth breaking up, and I ran away."

"Then," said the Lion, "you and I will go back to the place where the earth began to break up, and see what is the matter."

So the Lion put the little Rabbit on his back, and away they went like the wind. The other animals waited for them at the foot of the hill.

The Rabbit told the Lion when they were near the place where he slept, and the Lion saw just where the Rabbit had been sleeping.

He saw, too, the coconut that had fallen to the ground near by. Then the Lion said to the Rabbit, "It must have been the sound of the coconut falling to the ground that you heard. You foolish Rabbit!"

And the Lion ran back to the other animals, and told them all about it.

If it had not been for the wise King of Beasts, they might be running still.

A TALL TURNIP

an Appalachian tall tale collected by Ellis Credle

"All up and down the Blue Ridge Mountain the folks used to be scarified to poke their heads out-of-doors for fear of getting a stray bullet," said Hank Huggins. "That was when the Calloways and the Hugginses were a-doing some real feuding. Things have quieted down considerable since then. The two families have even come to speak to each other, and the young folks play ball and traipse around together somewhat. But there's some of the old feeling still left away down deep in every one of 'em. The Calloways are always trying to get ahead of the Hugginses in some way, and the Hugginses are just as set on outdistancing the Calloways, and usually they succeed—if I do say so as shouldn't, being a Huggins myself.

"When I looked out one day," Hank went on, "and saw old man Zeb Calloway a-planting turnips in a patch right next to my turnip patch, I suspected right away that he had a notion of outdoing me some way or other. And it turned out just as I'd figured it. He'd sent away to a mail-order house for some fancy turnip seed and he was allowing he'd raise some turnips that would make mine look like nubbins.

"'That's a game two can play at,' I said to myself, and I straddled my gray mule and took a trip down to Asheville and bought myself a package of turnip seed just as fancy as his. 'And it's not all in the seed either!' I said. 'I aim to out-cultivate, out-fertilize, and out-water old man Calloway ten to one.'

"I soon found out this took harder work than I cared for, so I settled down to specialize on one turnip. I did all my work on that one turnip and, folks, you ought to have seen it grow! Within a month the part that stuck out of the ground was up to my knee—not counting the leaves that struck me around the shoulders. By midsummer it was up to my waist, and by early fall it was head-high. It was a world's wonder, and folks from all over the hill country came to see it. Old man Calloway was that put out he wouldn't even stick his head out the door.

"Come fall, that turnip was still a-growing. I reckon it kept on even after winter set in but after the first freeze I was distracted by something else and forgot all about it. I had a flock of twenty-seven sheep disappear right off the face of the earth and I spent every spare minute a-hunting for 'em. All winter long I hunted for those sheep, on the high crags, through the valleys, and in the deep coves; but nary a sign of 'em did I see. After a while I gave 'em up for lost.

"One day in late spring, old man Calloway dropped in, pretending to condole with me. 'Those sheep of yours have fallen off a cliff, like as not,' he said, shaking his head mournfully. 'Or else they've starved to death during this bitter cold weather. Now if you'd spent more time a-building a sheepfold and less time on that pithy overgrown turnip, you would have been better off.'

"'Pithy!' I cried. 'That turnip's as sound as a dollar and you know it!'

"'Nothing of the kind. It's pithy, and worm-eaten, too. I was a-looking at it only yesterday and I saw a wormhole big enough for a man to crawl into. And when I struck it with the flat of my hand, it sounded as hollow as a barrel. You should have known a monstrous overgrown thing like that wouldn't be fit to eat.'

"That fairly outraged me. 'I'll cut into that turnip right now,' I said, snatching up an ax and setting off for the turnip patch, 'and you can see for yourself whether it's hollow or not!' The old man followed along at my heels and my wife, hearing the argument, came running out the door and traipsed along, too.

"I had to admit when I got to the patch that the turnip did look a bit seedy. It was big, there was no gainsaying that—nigh as big as a house—but it had a thin, frail look about it like it was all gone inside and might cave in any moment. The wormhole was there just as Zeb had claimed, and I'm jiggered if we couldn't hear a crunching chewing sound as if there was a whole army of worms in there hard at work.

"'Didn't I tell you so?' exclaimed the old man triumphantly. 'Pithy and full of worms—not fit for hogs to eat!'

"That made me really mad and I lifted my ax and split that turnip wide open.

"When it fell apart my wife let out a yell, 'Why, Hank, the sheep! There they are!'

"And sure enough, there they were, the whole flock of twenty-seven, all fat and sassy. There they'd been all winter long, sheltered from the cold, munching away, keeping plump and healthy on the insides of that turnip.

"'Hollow and pithy, was it?' I said, turning to old man Calloway. 'How many turnips on your side of the fence would have kept a flock of sheep alive during a whole winter?'

"Well, sir, Zeb never said a word. He saw I had him and he just turned and shambled off towards home."

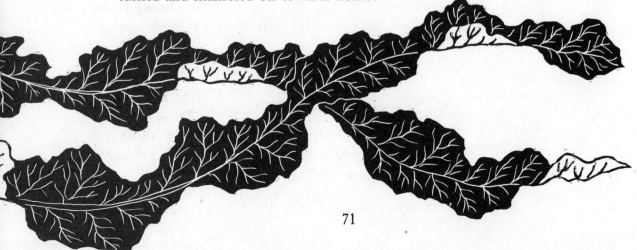

The Old Woman Who Lost Her Dumplings

a Japanese fairy tale retold by Lafcadio Hearn

Long, long ago there was a funny old woman, who liked to laugh and to make dumplings of rice-flour.

One day, while she was preparing some dumplings for dinner, she let one fall; and it rolled into a hole in the earthen floor of her little kitchen and disappeared. The old woman tried to reach it by putting her hand down the hole, and all at once the earth gave way, and the old woman fell in.

She fell quite a distance, but was not a bit hurt; and when she got up on her feet again, she saw that she was standing on a road, just like the road before her house. It was quite light down there; and she could see plenty of rice-fields, but no one in them. How all this happened, I cannot tell you. But it seems that the old woman had fallen into another country.

The road she had fallen upon sloped very much: so, after having looked for her dumpling in vain, she thought that it must have rolled farther away down the slope. She ran down the road to look, crying:

"My dumpling, my dumpling! Where is that dumpling of mine?"

After a little while she saw a stone *Fizó* standing by the roadside, and she said:

"O Lord *Fizó*, did you see my dumpling?" *Fizó* answered:

"Yes, I saw your dumpling rolling by me down the road. But you had better not go any farther, because there is a wicked *Oni* living down there, who eats people."

But the old woman only laughed, and ran on further down the road, crying: "My dumpling, my dumpling! Where is that dumpling of mine?" And she came to another statue of *Fizó*, and asked it:

72

"O kind Lord *Fizó*, did you see my dumpling?"

And *Fizó* said:

"Yes, I saw your dumpling go by a little while ago. But you must not run any further, because there is a wicked *Oni* down there, who eats people."

But she only laughed, and ran on, still crying out: "My dumpling, my dumpling! Where is that dumpling of mine?" And she came to a third *Fizó* and asked it:

"O dear Lord *Fizó*, did you see my dumpling?"

But *Fizó* said:

"Don't talk about your dumpling now. Here is the *Oni* coming. Squat down here behind my sleeve, and don't make any noise."

Presently the *Oni* came very close, and stopped and bowed to *Fizó*, and said:

"Good-day, *Fizó San!*"

Fizó said good-day, too, very politely.

Then the *Oni* suddenly snuffed the air two or three times in a suspicious way, and cried out: "*Fizó San, Fizó San!* I smell a smell of mankind somewhere—don't you?"

"Oh!" said *Fizó*, "perhaps you are mistaken."

"No, no!" said the *Oni* after snuffing the air again, "I smell a smell of mankind."

Then the old woman could not help laughing—"*Te-he-he!*"—and the *Oni* immediately reached down his big hairy hand behind *Fizó*'s sleeve, and pulled her out, still laughing, "*Te-he-he!*"

"Ah! ha!" cried the *Oni*.

Then *Fizó* said:

"What are you going to do with that good old woman? You must not hurt her."

"I won't," said the *Oni*. "But I will take her home with me to cook for us."

"*Te-he-he!*" laughed the old woman.

"Very well," said *Fizó*, "but you must really be kind to her. If you are not, I shall be very angry."

"I won't hurt her at all," promised the *Oni;* "and she will only have to do a little work for us every day. Good-by, *Fizó San.*"

Then the *Oni* took the old woman far down the road, till they came to a wide deep river, where there was a boat. He put her into the boat, and took her across the river to his house. It was a very large house. He led her at once into the kitchen, and told her to cook some dinner for himself and the other *Oni* who lived with him. And he gave her a small wooden rice-paddle, and said:

"You must always put only one grain of rice into the pot, and when you stir that one grain of rice in the water with this paddle, the grain will multiply until the pot is full."

So the old woman put just one rice-grain into the pot, as the *Oni* told her, and began to stir it with the paddle; and, as she stirred, the one grain became two,—then four,—then eight,—then sixteen, thirty-two, sixty-four, and so on. Every time she moved the paddle the rice increased in quantity; and in a few minutes the great pot was full.

After that, the funny old woman stayed a long time in the house of the *Oni*, and every day cooked food for all his friends. The *Oni* never hurt or frightened her, and her work was made quite easy by the magic paddle—although she had to cook a very, very great quantity of rice, because an *Oni* eats much more than any human being eats.

But she felt lonely, and always wished very much to go back to her own little house, and make her dumplings. And one day, when the *Oni* were all out somewhere, she thought she would try to run away.

She first took the magic paddle, and slipped it under her girdle; and then she went down to the river. No one saw her; and the boat was there. She got into it, and pushed off; and as she could row very well, she was soon far away from the shore.

But the river was very wide; and she had not rowed more than one-fourth of the way across, when the *Oni*, all of them, came back to the house.

They found that their cook was gone, and the magic paddle, too. They ran down to the river at once, and saw the old woman rowing away very fast.

Perhaps they could not swim: at all events they had no boat; and they thought the only way they could catch the funny old woman would be to drink up all the water of the river before she got to the other bank. So they knelt down, and began to drink so fast that before the old woman had got half way over, the water had become quite low.

But the old woman kept on rowing until the water had got so shallow that the *Oni* stopped drinking, and began to wade across. Then she dropped her oar, took the magic paddle from her girdle, and shook it at the *Oni*, and made such funny faces that the *Oni* all burst out laughing.

But the moment they laughed, they could not help throwing up all the water they had drunk, and so the river became full again. The *Oni* could not cross; and the funny old woman got safely over to the other side, and ran away up the road as fast as she could.

She never stopped running until she found herself at home again.

After that she was very happy; for she could make dumplings whenever she pleased. Besides, she had the magic paddle to make rice for her. She sold her dumplings to her neighbors and passengers, and in quite a short time she became rich.

The Squeaky Door

a Puerto Rican folk tale adapted
by Laura Simms

Once there was a little boy who lived with his grandma in a house in the forests of Puerto Rico. Every single night the little boy would get in his bed, pull the covers up over him, nestle his head in the pillow, and his old grandmother would come in.

And she'd say, "Tonight, when I shut the light, and it's dark and I close this squeaky door in your room, are you going to get scared and jump under the bed and start to cry?"

And the little boy would say, "No, not me."

So the grandma would say, "Good. I need my sleep. I'm so old."

The little boy would nestle in his pillow, and the grandma would say, "Are you going to be scared tonight?" And he would say, "No, not me."

"Good."

So she'd shut the light. And it would grow so dark. And then she'd close the squeaky door. *Squeeeeeak!*

And the little boy would jump out of his bed and get under the bed and start to cry.

And the grandma would come right back in, and she'd say, "You're driving me *crazy!* I'm mad, mad, *mad!*"

One night she got a good idea. She said, "Tonight I'll put a cat in the bed." So the boy got in the bed, and the cat got in the bed.

"Now," she said. "Are you going to be scared tonight?"

And he said, "No, not me."

"Good."

76

So she shut the light, and it grew so dark. And she closed that squeaky door. *Squeeeeeak!*

And the boy jumped under the bed and started to cry. And the cat jumped under the bed.

And the grandma came in, and she said, "You're driving me *crazy!* I'm mad, mad, *mad!*

"I know! I'll put a dog in the bed."

The next night the boy got in the bed, the cat got in the bed, and the dog got in the bed.

"Now," said the Grandma. "Are you going to be scared tonight?"

"No, not me."

"Good."

She shut the light. It grew so dark. And she closed that squeaky door. *Squeeeeeak!*

And the boy jumped under the bed and started to cry. And the cat jumped under the bed. And the dog jumped under the bed. And that grandma came in, and she said, "You're driving me *crazy.* I'm mad, mad, *mad.*

"I know! I'll put a pig in the bed."

The boy got in the bed, the cat got in the bed, the dog got in the bed, and the pig got in the bed. "Now, are you going to be scared tonight?"

"No, not me."

"Good."

So she closed the light. And it grew so dark. And she closed that squeaky door. *Squeeeeeak!*

And the boy jumped under the bed and started to cry. And the cat jumped under the bed. And the dog jumped under the bed. And the pig jumped under the bed. And that grandma came in, and she said, "I'm gonna pull out every hair in my head. You're driving me *crazy.* I'm mad, mad, *mad.*

"I know! I'll put a snake in the bed."

The boy got in the bed, the cat got in the bed, the dog got in the bed, the pig got in the bed, and the snake got in the bed.

"Now, are you going to be scared tonight?"

"No, not me."

"Good."

She shut the light. It grew dark. And she closed that squeaky door. *Squeeeeeak!*

And the boy got under the bed and cried. The cat got under the bed. The dog got under the bed. The pig got under the bed. And the snake slithered under the bed.

And that grandma came in, and she said, "I'm gonna pull out every hair in my head. You're driving me *crazy*. I'm mad, mad, *mad*. I know! Why didn't I think of this before? I'll put a horse in the bed."

The boy got in the bed, the cat got in the bed, the dog got in the bed, the pig got in the bed, the snake got in the bed, and the horse got in the bed. "Now, are you going to be scared tonight?"

"No, not me."

"Good."

She shut the light. It grew dark. And she closed that squeaky door. *Squeeeeeak!*

And the boy jumped under the bed and cried. And the cat jumped under the bed. And the dog jumped under the bed. And the pig jumped under the bed. And the snake slithered under the bed. And the horse jumped under the bed.

You know what happened? The bed collapsed. And the house fell apart. They had to move to a new house, and in this house the door did not squeak. And they lived happily ever after.

A Wolf and Little Daughter

an American black folk tale
told by Virginia Hamilton

One day Little Daughter was pickin some flowers. There was a fence around the house she lived in with her papa. Papa didn't want Little Daughter to run in the forest, where there were wolves. He told Little Daughter never to go out the gate alone.

"Oh, I won't, Papa," said Little Daughter.

One mornin her papa had to go away for somethin. And Little Daughter thought she'd go huntin for flowers. She just thought it wouldn't harm anythin to peep through the gate. And that's what she did. She saw a wild yellow flower so near to the gate that she stepped outside and picked it.

Little Daughter was outside the fence now. She saw another pretty flower. She skipped over and got it, held it in her hand. It smelled sweet. She saw another and she got it, too. Put it with the others. She was makin a pretty bunch to put in her vase for the table. And so Little Daughter got farther and farther away from the cabin. She picked the flowers, and the whole time she sang a sweet song.

All at once Little Daughter heard a noise. She looked up and saw a great big wolf. The wolf said to her, in a low, gruff voice, said, "Sing that sweetest, goodest song again."

So the little child sang it, sang,

"Tray-bla, tray-bla, cum qua, kimo."

And, *pit-a-pat, pit-a-pat, pit-a-pat, pit-a-pat,* Little Daughter tiptoed toward the gate. She's goin back home. But she hears big and heavy, PIT-A-PAT, PIT-A-PAT, comin behind her. And there's the wolf. He says, "Did you move?" in a gruff voice.

Little Daughter says, "Oh, no, dear wolf, what occasion have I to move?"

"Well, sing that sweetest, goodest song again," says the wolf. Little Daughter sang it:

"Tray-bla, tray-bla, cum qua, kimo."

And the wolf is gone again.

The child goes back some more, *pit-a-pat, pit-a-pat, pit-a-pat,* softly on tippy-toes toward the gate.

But she soon hears very loud, PIT-A-PAT, PIT-A-PAT, comin behind her. And there is the great big wolf, and he says to her, says, "I think you moved."

"Oh, no, dear wolf," Little Daughter tells him, "what occasion have I to move?"

So he says, "Sing that sweetest, goodest song again."

Little Daughter begins:

"Tray-bla, tray-bla, tray-bla, cum qua kimo."

The wolf is gone.
But, PIT-A-PAT, PIT-A-PAT, PIT-A-PAT, comin on behind her.
There's the wolf. He says to her, says, "You moved."
She says, "Oh, no, dear wolf, what occasion have I to move?"
"Sing that sweetest, goodest song again," says the big, bad wolf.
She sang:

"Tray bla-tray, tray bla-tray, tray-bla-cum qua, kimo."

The wolf is gone again.
And she, Little Daughter, *pit-a-pat, pit-a-pat, pit-a-pat*tin away
home. She is so close to the gate now. And this time she hears PIT-A-
PAT, PIT-A-PAT, PIT-A-PAT comin on *quick* behind her.
Little Daughter slips inside the gate. She shuts it—CRACK!
PLICK!—right in that big, bad wolf's face.
She sweetest, goodest safe!

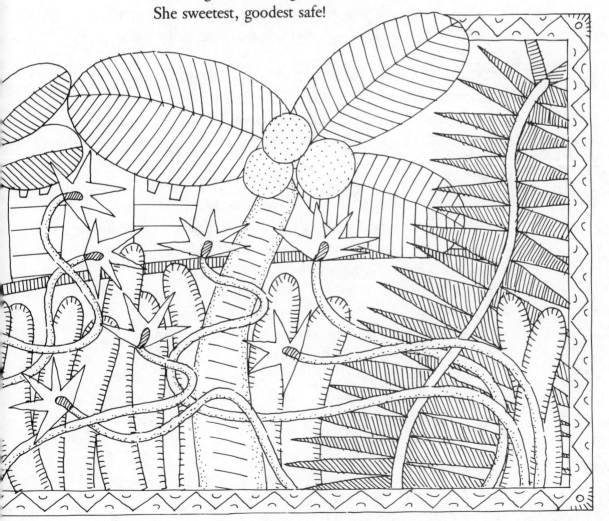

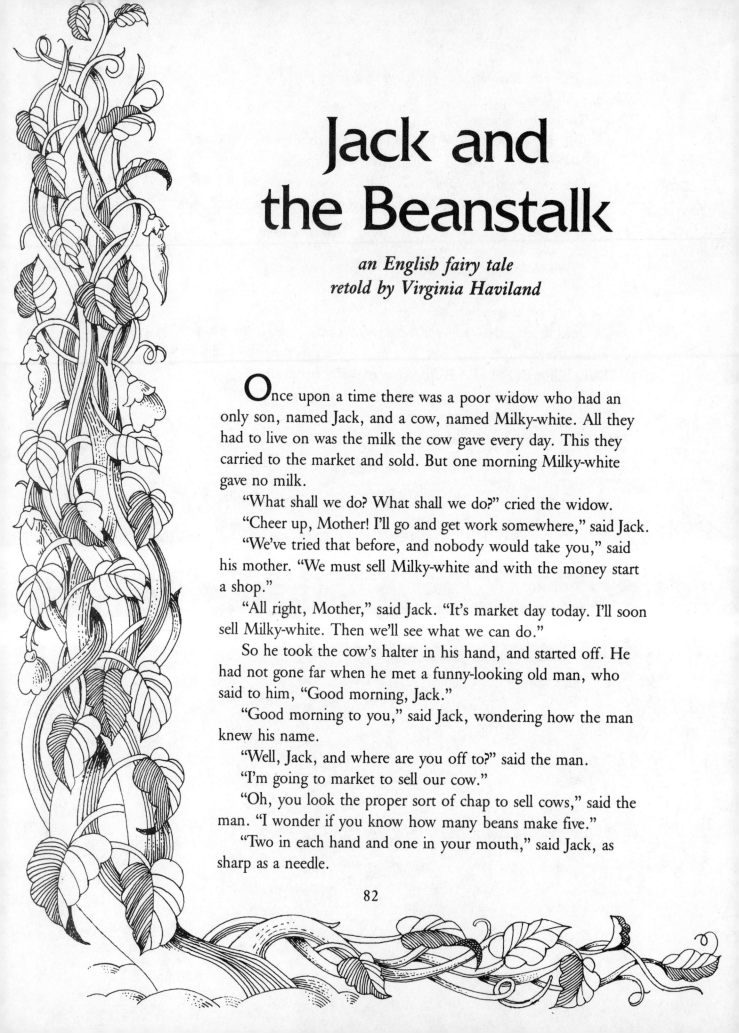

Jack and the Beanstalk

an English fairy tale
retold by Virginia Haviland

Once upon a time there was a poor widow who had an only son, named Jack, and a cow, named Milky-white. All they had to live on was the milk the cow gave every day. This they carried to the market and sold. But one morning Milky-white gave no milk.

"What shall we do? What shall we do?" cried the widow.

"Cheer up, Mother! I'll go and get work somewhere," said Jack.

"We've tried that before, and nobody would take you," said his mother. "We must sell Milky-white and with the money start a shop."

"All right, Mother," said Jack. "It's market day today. I'll soon sell Milky-white. Then we'll see what we can do."

So he took the cow's halter in his hand, and started off. He had not gone far when he met a funny-looking old man, who said to him, "Good morning, Jack."

"Good morning to you," said Jack, wondering how the man knew his name.

"Well, Jack, and where are you off to?" said the man.

"I'm going to market to sell our cow."

"Oh, you look the proper sort of chap to sell cows," said the man. "I wonder if you know how many beans make five."

"Two in each hand and one in your mouth," said Jack, as sharp as a needle.

"Right you are," said the man, "and here they are, the very beans themselves." He pulled out of his pocket a number of strange-looking beans. "Since you are so sharp," said he, "I don't mind trading with you—your cow for these beans."

"Go along!" said Jack.

"Ah! You don't know what these beans are," said the man. "If you plant them at night, by morning the stalks will be right up to the sky."

"Really?" said Jack. "You don't say so."

"Yes, that is so, and if it doesn't turn out to be true, you can have your cow back."

"Right," said Jack. He handed over Milky-white's halter and pocketed the beans.

Back home went Jack. It was not dusk by the time he got to his door.

"Back already, Jack?" said his mother. "I see you haven't got Milky-white, so you've sold her. How much did you get for her?"

"You'll never guess, Mother," said Jack.

"No, you don't say so! Good boy! Five pounds? Ten? Fifteen? No, it can't be twenty!"

"I told you you couldn't guess. What do you say to these beans? They're magical—plant them at night and . . ."

"What!" said Jack's mother. "Have you been such a fool as to give away my Milky-white for a set of dry beans? Take that! Take that! Take that!" and she gave him three hard slaps. "As for your magic beans, here they go out of the window. Now off with you to bed. Not a drop shall you drink and not a bite shall you swallow this very night."

So Jack went upstairs to his little room in the attic. Sad and sorry he was, to be sure.

At last he dropped off to sleep.

When he woke up, his room looked very strange! The sun was shining, yet the room seemed dark and shadowy. Jack jumped up and ran to the window. What do you think he saw? Why, the beans his mother had thrown out of the window into the garden had sprung up into a big beanstalk. It went up and up and up till it reached the sky. The old man had spoken the truth after all.

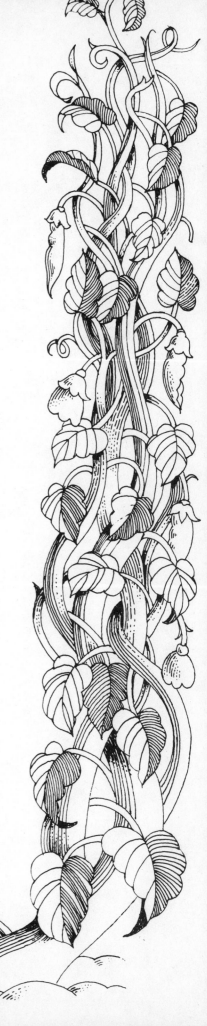

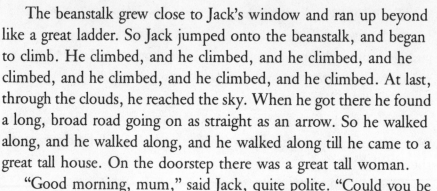

The beanstalk grew close to Jack's window and ran up beyond like a great ladder. So Jack jumped onto the beanstalk, and began to climb. He climbed, and he climbed, and he climbed, and he climbed, and he climbed, and he climbed, and he climbed. At last, through the clouds, he reached the sky. When he got there he found a long, broad road going on as straight as an arrow. So he walked along, and he walked along, and he walked along till he came to a great tall house. On the doorstep there was a great tall woman.

"Good morning, mum," said Jack, quite polite. "Could you be so kind as to give me some breakfast?" For he hadn't had anything to eat the night before, you know. He was as hungry as a hunter.

"It's breakfast you want, is it?" said the great tall woman. "It's breakfast you'll *be* if you don't move off from here. My man is a giant, and there's nothing he likes better than boys broiled on toast. You'd better be moving on or he'll soon be coming."

"Oh! Please, mum, do give me something to eat, mum. I've had nothing since yesterday morning, really and truly, mum," said Jack. "I may as well be broiled as die of hunger."

Well, the giant's wife was not half so bad after all. She took Jack into the kitchen, and gave him a chunk of bread and cheese and jug of milk. But Jack hadn't half finished these when—*thump! thump! thump!*—the whole house began to tremble with the noise of someone coming.

"Goodness gracious me! It's my old man," said the giant's wife. "What on earth shall I do? Come along quick and jump in here." She bundled Jack into the oven, just as the giant came in.

He was a big man, to be sure. At his belt he had three calves strung up by the heels. He threw them down on the table and said, "Here, wife, broil me two of these for breakfast. Ah! What's this I smell? . . .

> *"Fee–fi–fo–fum.*
> *I smell the blood of an Englishman!*
> *Be he alive, or be he dead,*
> *I'll grind his bones to make my bread."*

"Nonsense, dear," said his wife. "You're dreaming. Or perhaps you smell the scraps of that little boy you liked so much for yesterday's dinner. Here, go wash and tidy up. By the time you come back your breakfast will be ready for you."

Off the giant went. Jack was just going to jump out of the oven and run away when the woman told him not to. "Wait till he's asleep," said she. "He always has a nap after breakfast."

The giant had his breakfast. After that he went to a big chest and took out of it two bags of gold. Down he sat and counted till at last his head began to nod. He began to snore till the whole house shook again.

Then Jack crept out on tiptoe from his oven. As he passed the giant, he took one of the bags of gold under his arm. Off he ran till he came to the beanstalk. He threw down the bag of gold, which of course fell into his mother's garden. He climbed down and climbed down till at last he got home. He told his mother what had happened and showed her the gold.

"Well, Mother," he said, "wasn't I right about the beans? They *are* really magical, you see."

They lived on the bag of gold for some time, but at last they came to the end of it. Jack made up his mind to try his luck once more at the top of the beanstalk. So one fine morning he rose early and got onto the beanstalk. He climbed, and he climbed, and he climbed, and he climbed, and he climbed, and he climbed. At last he came out on to the road again and up to the great tall house he had been to before. There, sure enough, was the great tall woman standing on the doorstep.

"Good morning, mum," said Jack, as bold as brass. "Could you be so good as to give me something to eat?"

"Go away, my boy," said the great tall woman, "or else my man will eat you up for breakfast. But aren't you the boy who came here once before? Do you know, that very day my man missed one of his bags of gold!"

"That's strange, mum," said Jack. "I dare say I could tell you something about that. But I'm so hungry I can't speak till I've had something to eat."

Well, the great tall woman was so curious that she took him in and gave him something to eat. But he had scarcely begun munching it, as slowly as he could, when—*thump! thump! thump!*—they heard the giant's footstep, and his wife again hid Jack in the oven.

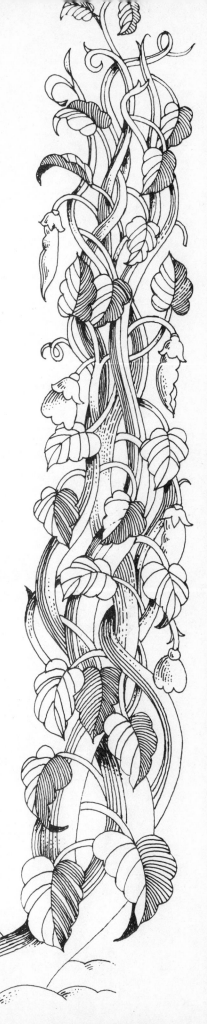

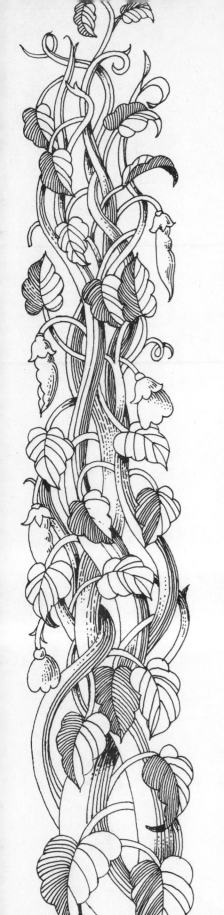

Everything happened as it did before. In came the giant, roaring "Fee-fi-fo-fum," and had his breakfast of three broiled oxen. Then he ordered, "Wife, bring me the hen that lays the golden eggs."

So she brought it. Her husband said, "Lay," and the hen laid an egg all of gold. But then the giant began to nod his head and to snore till the house shook.

Now Jack crept out of the oven on tiptoe and caught hold of the golden hen. He was off before you could say "Jack Robinson." This time, the giant woke—because the hen gave a cackle. Just as Jack got out of the house, he heard the giant calling, "Wife, wife, what have you done with my golden hen?"

And the wife said, "Why, my dear?"

But that was all Jack heard, for he rushed off to the beanstalk and climbed down in a flash. When he got home he showed his mother the wonderful hen, and said, "Lay!" to it. It laid a golden egg every time he said, "Lay!"

Well, Jack was not content. It wasn't very long before he decided to try his luck again up there at the top of the beanstalk. One fine morning he rose early and stepped onto the beanstalk. He climbed, and he climbed, and he climbed, and he climbed, till he came to the very top. This time he knew better than to go straight to the giant's house. When he came near it, he waited behind a bush till he saw the giant's wife come out with a pail to get some water. Then he crept into the house and hid in a copper tub. He hadn't been there long when he heard *thump! thump! thump!* as before. In walked the giant and his wife.

"Fee-fi-fo-fum, I smell the blood of an Englishman!" cried out the giant. "I smell him, wife, I smell him."

"Do you, my dear?" said the wife. "Well then, if it's the little rogue that stole your gold and the hen that laid the golden eggs, he's sure to have got into the oven." And they both rushed to the oven.

But Jack wasn't there, luckily. The giant's wife said, "There you are again with your fee-fi-fo-fum! Why, of course, it's the boy you caught last night that I've just broiled for your breakfast. How forgetful I am! And how careless you are not to know the difference between alive and dead, after all these years."

So the giant sat down to his breakfast. Every now and then he would mutter, "Well I could have sworn . . ." And he'd get up and search the larder and the cupboards and everything. Only, luckily, he didn't think of the tub.

After breakfast, the giant called out, "Wife, wife, bring me my golden harp." So she brought it and put it on the table before him. "Sing!" he ordered, and the golden harp sang most beautifully. It went on singing till the giant fell asleep and began to snore like thunder.

Jack now got out of the tub very quietly and crept like a mouse over to the table. Up he crawled, caught hold of the golden harp, and dashed with it toward the door. But the harp called out quite loudly, "Master! Master!"

The giant woke up just in time to see Jack running off with his harp.

Jack ran as fast as he could. The giant came rushing after, and would soon have caught him, only Jack had a head start and knew where he was going. When he got to the beanstalk, the giant was not more than twenty yards away. Suddenly Jack disappeared. When the giant came to the end of the road, he saw Jack below climbing down for dear life.

Well, the giant didn't like to trust himself to such a ladder. He stood and waited, so Jack got another start.

But the harp cried out again, "Master! Master!"

The giant swung himself down onto the beanstalk, which shook with his weight. Down climbed Jack, and after him climbed the giant.

Jack climbed down, and climbed down, and climbed down till he was very nearly home. Then he called out, "Mother! Mother! Bring me an ax, bring me an ax!" His mother rushed out with the ax in her hand. When she came to the beanstalk, she stood stock-still with fright. There was the giant with his legs just through the clouds.

Jack jumped down, took the ax, and chopped at the beanstalk, almost cutting it in two. The giant felt the beanstalk shake, so he stopped to see what the matter was. Then Jack chopped again. The beanstalk was cut in two. It began to topple over. Down crashed the giant, and that was the end of him!

Jack gave his mother the golden harp. With the magical harp and the golden eggs, Jack and his mother became very rich. Jack married a Princess, and they all lived happily ever after.

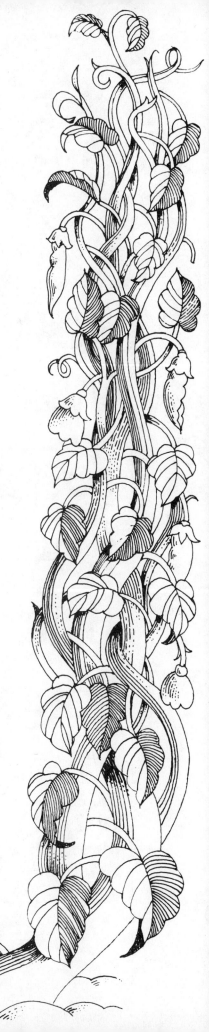

Why Leopard Has Black Spots

a story from
the Dan people
of Liberia
told by
Won-Ldy Paye
edited by
Margaret H. Lippert

One day there was a spider. He was a great farmer. He lived in a village with a leopard and a deer. Spider had a BIG garden. He had so much food in his garden that every evening Spider would call Leopard and Deer and cook food for them.

But one day Spider went to his garden and noticed something was different. "Something is missing," he thought. Day after day things seemed to be missing.

At first he didn't care, because his garden was so big. But then it began to make him mad. One day he looked at his garden and said, "I saw a pumpkin here last night. Why is the pumpkin not here this morning?"

The next day he said, "I thought I saw a big cucumber here. Why is it not there?"

Spider began to check his farm very carefully. He was sure there were 98 tomatoes. But when he came back, there were 95. Man, this was really getting to Spider! He told his friends that his tomatoes were missing, but they laughed at him. "You want to tell me I'm not able to count right?" Spider asked.

Spider began to mark every single thing in his garden. Sometimes when he checked, instead of going from 1-2-3-4, the numbers went 1-3-5-7. And Spider said, "Something must be wrong!"

Spider went to Deer's hut. "Are you the one who is stealing from my garden all the time?"

88

Deer went: "Oh, no, no, no, no, no, no, no. Not me. You call for me every evening. You provide me dinner. Why should I go steal from your garden?"

Spider said, "I don't like stealing. I hope it's not you."

Deer said, "It's not me."

Spider went to Leopard. "Leopard, please be honest with me. Are you stealing from my garden?"

Leopard said, "No, I like meats. I really don't like too much veg-e-table. I am only eating veg-e-tables because you invite us to eat with you. You provide it for us."

Spider said, "Okay."

The vegetables kept on disappearing. Spider started to get really mad.

Spider went to Deer's house again. "Are you the one who's stealing from my garden?"

Deer said, "N-n-n-n-n-n-n-no!"

Spider said, "How come you're going 'n-n-no' like that?"

Deer said, "B-b-b-b-but that's the w-w-w-way I t-t-t-t-talk."

Spider said, "What! How come you don't talk like that all the time?"

Deer said, "When I'm m-m-m-m-mad, I t-t-t-t-talk like this." So Deer started pretending that he was mad, and that's why he was talking like this. Spider was really surprised because he never heard Deer talk like this before.

Then Spider went back to Leopard's house. "Are you the one who is stealing from my garden?"

Leopard said, "I told you I like meat. I don't like veg-e-table too much. So go ask Deer."

This time when Spider came to Deer, Deer said, "Here's what you should do: Go and dig a big hole in front of the entrance to the garden, and put a lot a fire in it and build it up. Cover it with a lot of dry branches. Let the fire burn way down. When the person who is stealing from your garden goes through the entrance, they'll fall in the fire. The next day when you come, you will see them."

So Spider went and dug the hole, and lit a fire in the bottom of it. He let the fire burn way down to red-hot coals, and then he covered the hole with dry branches, just as Deer said.

But Deer knew where the hole was, because Deer was the one who told Spider the trick. So Deer went around the hole and went into Spider's garden and stole other things. Then he ran to Leopard's house, and he said, "Spider called you."

Leopard said, "Where's Spider?"

Deer said, "Spider is in his garden."

So Leopard ran to the garden. When he went through the entrance to the garden, Leopard fell in the hole. And Leopard started to get burned.

Deer ran to Spider. Deer said, "Come! Come! Come! Come! I saw the person who is stealing from the garden all the time. We should keep this old Leopard down there fighting and trying to get up."

Spider shouted to Leopard: "You've been stealing from my garden all the time! Now I've got you!"

Leopard said, "I don't know what you're talking about. I just want to get out of this fire."

Spider said, "Why have you been lying to me all the time? Every time you said you are not the one. Now my trap has caught you."

Leopard said, "I don't know what you're talking about. I just want to get out of this fire."

So Leopard leaped high. Ahhh, he got out of the fire. So Leopard said, "What is all this about?"

Spider said, "Deer told me I should play this trick. And now I find out who's been stealing."

And Leopard said, "But how come Deer came to me and said that you called me to the garden?"

Spider looked at Deer and said, "Did I send you to go get Leopard?"

The Deer said, "No."

Spider said, "Ohhhh, so it's you, Deer, who's been stealing from the garden all the time."

Leopard said, "WHAT! You did that! You did this to me? Because of your trick, I've got all these black spots on my skin because I got burned in the fire!"

Since that day, all the leopards we see have black, black, black spots all over their skin.

"You did this, Deer? Because of these black spots, anywhere I see you," Leopard said, "I'M GOING TO EAT YOU!" So Deer ran away. And Leopard ran after him.

Since that day, no matter how much you train the deer, no matter how much you train the leopard, don't put them together, because Leopard is sure going to eat Deer.

That's why Deer and Leopard aren't friends now, and that's why Leopard has black spots all over his skin.

The Black Cat

an American folk tale
retold by Margaret H. Lippert

The following story is designed to be told by a storyteller who is simultaneously drawing the accompanying diagram on a large piece of white paper with a black crayon or marker (so that a black cat will appear). Telling this story is more effective than reading it aloud, because the picture must be drawn as the story is told.

The story is very easy to learn. The plot follows the parts of the diagram, which are drawn sequentially, so the sequence of the story can be remembered by following the sequence of the drawings.

The text below can be freely adapted by the teacher, but the elements of the drawing must remain the same (square house, rectangular doors, round windows, triangular chimneys, "S" tail, four legs, etc.).

Once upon a time, there was a boy named Tommy. Here's a "T," for "Tommy":

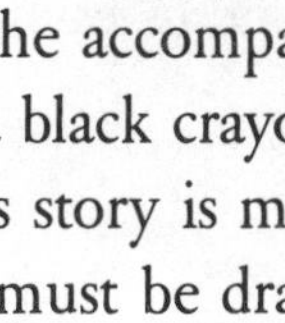

T

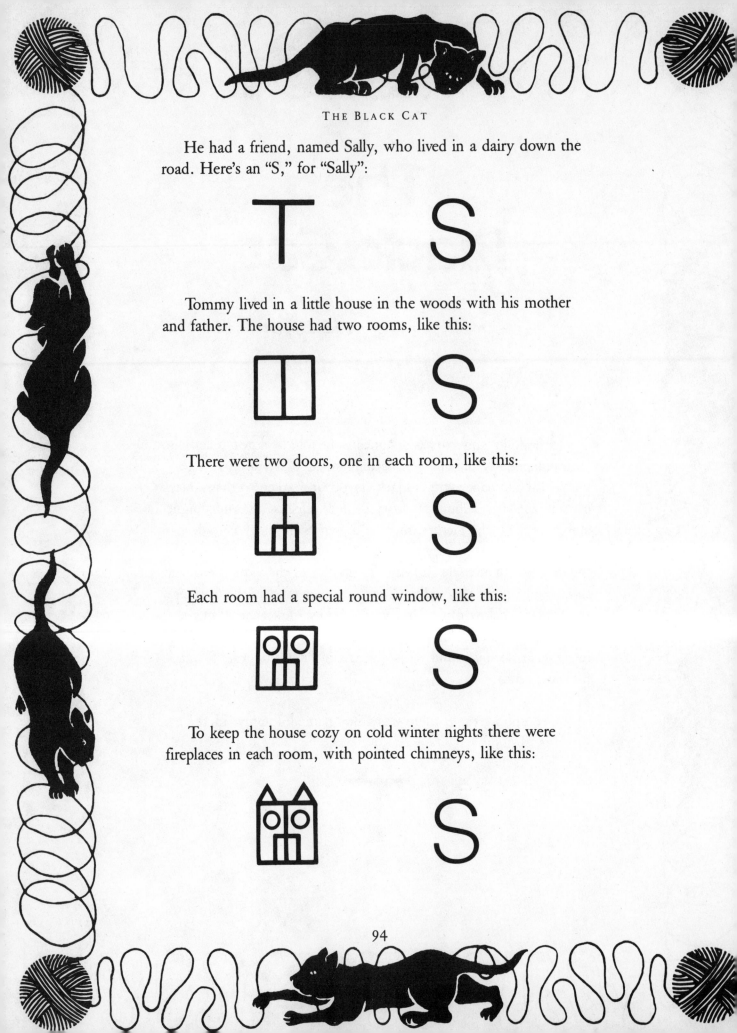

THE BLACK CAT

He had a friend, named Sally, who lived in a dairy down the road. Here's an "S," for "Sally":

T S

Tommy lived in a little house in the woods with his mother and father. The house had two rooms, like this:

S

There were two doors, one in each room, like this:

S

Each room had a special round window, like this:

S

To keep the house cozy on cold winter nights there were fireplaces in each room, with pointed chimneys, like this:

S

Outside the front door, grass grew thick and tall, like this:

 S

One day, Tommy's mother sent him to buy some cream from Sally. He walked along the road to the dairy.

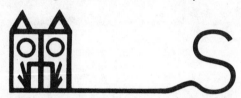

"The cream is down in the cellar," said Sally. "Would you like to come down with me?" Tommy and Sally went down the steps to the cellar.

"Shhh," said Sally. "I have a surprise for you." She pointed to a box in the corner. Tommy saw nothing in it but an old, torn blanket. Then he heard "mew, mew, mew." He saw the blanket moving, and a tiny head poked out. "Kittens!" he whispered.

"Yes," said Sally, "but the mother left this morning and has not come back. I am afraid she may be lost or hurt."

"I'll look for her on my way home," said Tommy. "What color is she?"

"She's black, so she may be hard to see in the woods," said Sally. "I'll come with you. With two of us looking, we're more likely to find her." Sally filled a pitcher with cream. Then she led Tommy up the steps.

But just as Sally reached the top step, she stumbled and fell. She and Tommy both went crashing down the steps. The pitcher broke and cream splashed all over the floor.

The kittens mewed frantically. "We must find their mother soon," said Sally. "I will clean up the cream later." She found a jar with a lid and filled it with fresh cream. Then she wrapped it in some cloth to keep it cool. Tommy and Sally went back up the steps. This time, they held on to the bannister.

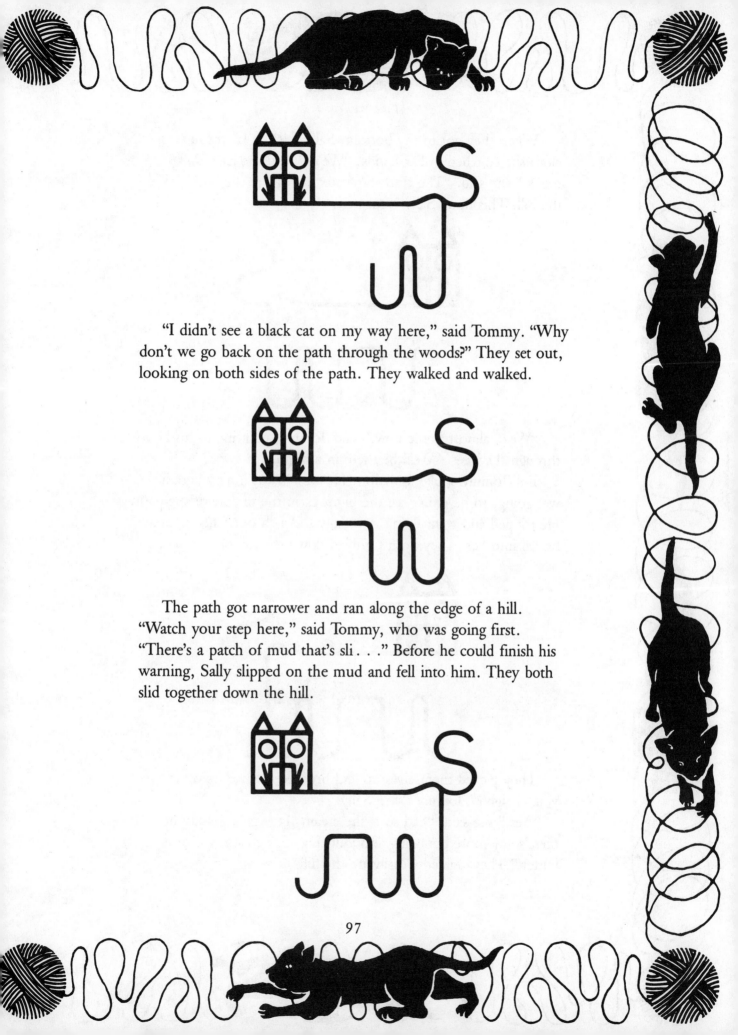

"I didn't see a black cat on my way here," said Tommy. "Why don't we go back on the path through the woods?" They set out, looking on both sides of the path. They walked and walked.

The path got narrower and ran along the edge of a hill. "Watch your step here," said Tommy, who was going first. "There's a patch of mud that's sli . . ." Before he could finish his warning, Sally slipped on the mud and fell into him. They both slid together down the hill.

When they got to the bottom, Sally felt the jar through the cloth she clutched in her hands. "We're lucky the jar didn't break," she said. "The cloth protected it." They climbed back up the hill. This time, Sally went first.

"We're almost home now," said Tommy, pointing to his house through the trees. "We'll be there in a minute or two."

But Tommy spoke too soon. He wasn't watching where he was going, so he didn't see the big rock in the middle of the path. He tripped and went flying into Sally. "Watch out," he called as he fell into her. They both tumbled down the hill once more.

They picked themselves up and brushed themselves off. "Are you all right?" Tommy asked Sally.

"Yes," she said, "and so is the cream. Let's go carefully now. If there's any more bouncing and jouncing, this cream will turn into butter." They walked wearily up the hill.

Tommy and Sally looked both ways before they crossed the road. "We can cross now," said Tommy. "There are no cars."

"And no black cat," said Sally. Sadly they crossed the road. They hadn't found the mother cat. Where could she be? They went up the path to Tommy's house and suddenly Sally squealed, "Look Tommy! Look who's standing there as if she's been waiting all morning just for us to bring her some sweet, fresh cream."

"Why, there she is!" shouted Tommy. "We found her! THE BLACK CAT!"

The Elves and the Shoemaker

a German fairy tale
by the Brothers Grimm
adapted by Amy Ehrlich

There was once a shoemaker who became poorer and poorer as the years went by. At last he had leather enough only for one pair of shoes. In the evening he cut out the pattern and then he went to sleep.

The next morning he took up a needle and thread, meaning to sew the shoes. But there they stood, neatly sewn and finished on his table. The shoemaker could not believe his eyes. Not a stitch was out of place and the work was better than any he had ever seen.

As he held the shoes, marveling at them, a customer entered the shop. He was so pleased with the shoes that he paid far more than the ordinary price, and the shoemaker was able to buy leather for two pairs more.

He cut them out in the evening, and the next morning prepared to begin work. But there was no need for it because the shoes had already been made and were as well stitched and handsome as the other pair. The first two customers who came into his shop bought them for a good price. And this time the shoemaker was able to buy leather enough for four pairs.

Early the next morning the four pairs of shoes were finished as before. And so it went. What the shoemaker cut out at night was finished in the morning, and customers were never lacking. Soon the shoemaker became a wealthy man.

Always he wondered about the skill of the work, and one evening not long before Christmas he said to his wife, "How would it be if we were to sit up tonight to see who has been helping us these many months?"

She agreed at once and so they did not go to bed, but lit a candle and hid themselves in a corner of the room. Just at midnight two tiny little men came and sat down at the shoemaker's table. They wore no clothes and said not a single word, but immediately began to work. They stitched and hammered and sewed so neatly and quickly that the shoemaker was amazed. As soon as everything was finished and stood upon the table, they ran quickly away.

"The little men have made us rich and I think we ought to thank them," said the shoemaker's wife in the morning. "They ran about with nothing on and must freeze with cold. Now I shall sew them tiny shirts and pants and coats and knit them caps and socks. And you must make them each a pair of shoes."

The shoemaker and his wife worked hard all day and had everything ready by evening. Then they hid themselves to see how the little men would receive their presents.

At midnight the two came back into the room and sat down at the table. But instead of leather cut out and waiting, they found the wonderful little clothes.

First the little men were surprised and then they were delighted. They put on the shirts and pants, the coats and socks and caps, and they buckled the tiny shoes upon their feet. When they were done they ran their hands up and down the pretty clothes and admired each other, singing:

> *"Now that we're boys so fine and neat,*
> *Why cobble more for others' feet?"*

They hopped and danced about the shoemaker's shop, leaping over chairs and tables and then out the door. From this night on the two little men came back no more, but the shoemaker continued to do well as long as he lived and had good luck in all he attempted.

A Day When
FROGS WEAR SHOES

a story by Ann Cameron

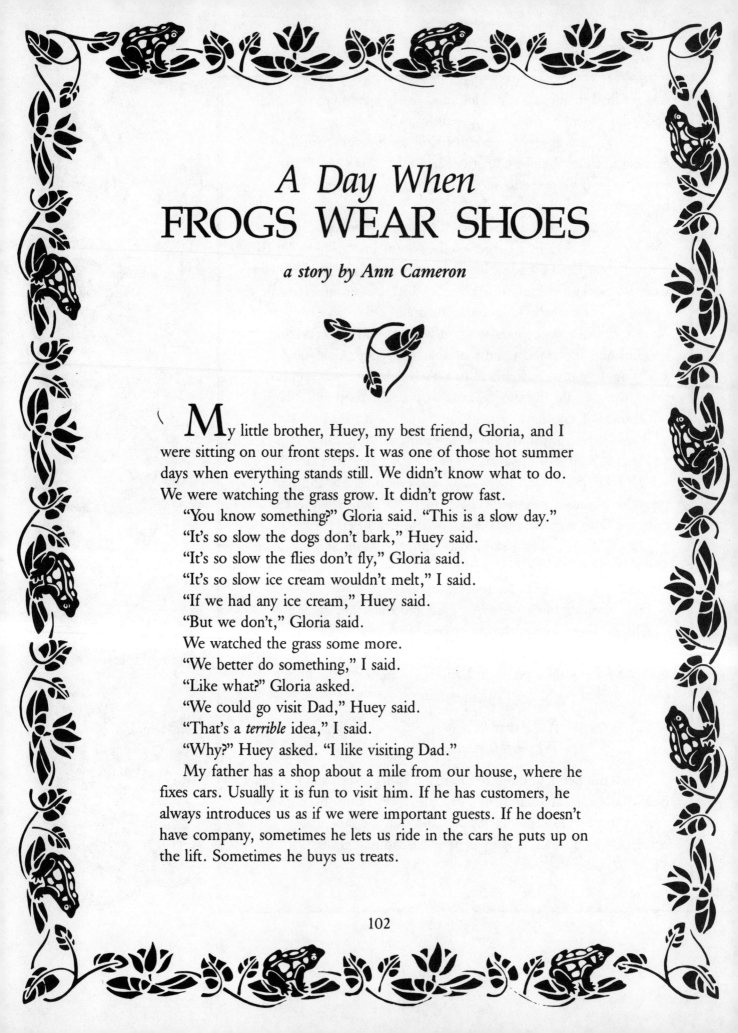

My little brother, Huey, my best friend, Gloria, and I were sitting on our front steps. It was one of those hot summer days when everything stands still. We didn't know what to do. We were watching the grass grow. It didn't grow fast.

"You know something?" Gloria said. "This is a slow day."

"It's so slow the dogs don't bark," Huey said.

"It's so slow the flies don't fly," Gloria said.

"It's so slow ice cream wouldn't melt," I said.

"If we had any ice cream," Huey said.

"But we don't," Gloria said.

We watched the grass some more.

"We better do something," I said.

"Like what?" Gloria asked.

"We could go visit Dad," Huey said.

"That's a *terrible* idea," I said.

"Why?" Huey asked. "I like visiting Dad."

My father has a shop about a mile from our house, where he fixes cars. Usually it is fun to visit him. If he has customers, he always introduces us as if we were important guests. If he doesn't have company, sometimes he lets us ride in the cars he puts up on the lift. Sometimes he buys us treats.

"Huey," I said, "usually, visiting Dad is a good idea. Today, it's a dangerous idea."

"Why?" Gloria said.

"Because we're bored," I said. "My dad hates it when people are bored. He says the world is so interesting nobody should ever be bored."

"I see," Gloria said, as if she didn't.

"So we'll go see him," Huey said, "and we just won't tell him we're bored. We're bored, but we won't tell him."

"Just so you remember that!" I said.

"Oh, I'll remember," Huey said.

Huey was wearing his angel look. When he has that look, you know he'll never remember anything.

Huey and I put on sweat bands. Gloria put on dark glasses. We started out.

The sun shined up at us from the sidewalks. Even the shadows on the street were hot as blankets.

Huey picked up a stick and scratched it along the sidewalk. "Oh, we're bored," he muttered. "Bored, bored, bored, bored, bored!"

"Huey!" I yelled. I wasn't bored anymore. I was nervous. Finally we reached a sign:

RALPH'S CAR HOSPITAL
PUNCTURES
RUST
DENTS & BASHES
BAD BRAKES
BAD BREAKS
UNUSUAL COMPLAINTS

That's my dad's sign. My dad is Ralph.

The parking lot had three cars in it. Dad was inside the shop, lifting the hood of another car. He didn't have any customers with him, so we didn't get to shake hands and feel like visiting mayors or congressmen.

"Hi, Dad," I said.

"Hi!" my dad said.

"We're—" Huey said.

I didn't trust Huey. I stepped on his foot.

"We're on a hike," I said.

"Well, nice of you to stop by," my father said. "If you want, you can stay awhile and help me."

"O.K.," we said.

So Huey sorted nuts and bolts. Gloria shined fenders with a rag. I held a new windshield wiper while my dad put it on a car window.

"Nice work, Huey and Julian and Gloria!" my dad said when we were done.

And then he sent us to the store across the street to buy paper cups and ice cubes and a can of frozen lemonade.

We mixed the lemonade in the shop. Then we sat out under the one tree by the side of the driveway and drank all of it.

"Good lemonade!" my father said. "So what are you kids going to do now?"

"Oh, hike!" I said.

"You know," my father answered, "I'm surprised at you kids picking a hot day like today for a hike. The ground is so hot. On a day like this, frogs wear shoes!"

"They do?" Huey said.

"Especially if they go hiking," my father said. "Of course, a lot of frogs, on a day like this, would stay home. So I wonder why you kids are hiking."

Sometimes my father notices too much. Then he gets yellow lights shining in his eyes, asking you to tell the whole truth. That's when I know to look at my feet.

"Oh," I said, "we *like* hiking."

But Gloria didn't know any better. She looked into my father's eyes. "Really," she said, "this wasn't a real hike. We came to see you."

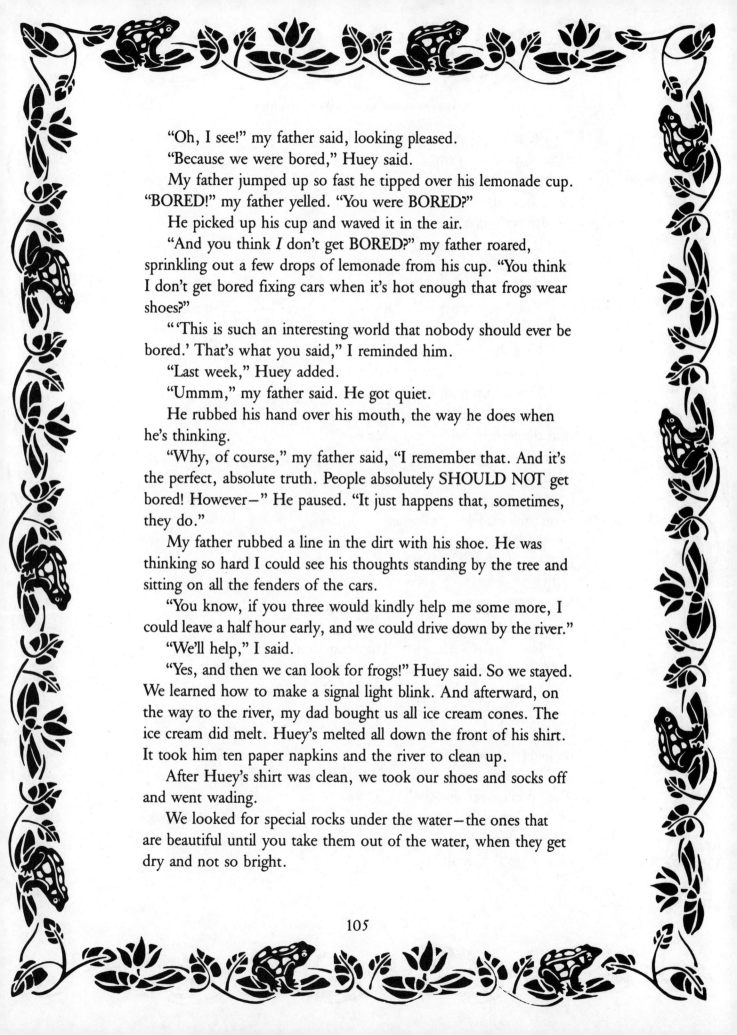

"Oh, I see!" my father said, looking pleased.

"Because we were bored," Huey said.

My father jumped up so fast he tipped over his lemonade cup. "BORED!" my father yelled. "You were BORED?"

He picked up his cup and waved it in the air.

"And you think *I* don't get BORED?" my father roared, sprinkling out a few drops of lemonade from his cup. "You think I don't get bored fixing cars when it's hot enough that frogs wear shoes?"

" 'This is such an interesting world that nobody should ever be bored.' That's what you said," I reminded him.

"Last week," Huey added.

"Ummm," my father said. He got quiet.

He rubbed his hand over his mouth, the way he does when he's thinking.

"Why, of course," my father said, "I remember that. And it's the perfect, absolute truth. People absolutely SHOULD NOT get bored! However—" He paused. "It just happens that, sometimes, they do."

My father rubbed a line in the dirt with his shoe. He was thinking so hard I could see his thoughts standing by the tree and sitting on all the fenders of the cars.

"You know, if you three would kindly help me some more, I could leave a half hour early, and we could drive down by the river."

"We'll help," I said.

"Yes, and then we can look for frogs!" Huey said. So we stayed. We learned how to make a signal light blink. And afterward, on the way to the river, my dad bought us all ice cream cones. The ice cream did melt. Huey's melted all down the front of his shirt. It took him ten paper napkins and the river to clean up.

After Huey's shirt was clean, we took our shoes and socks off and went wading.

We looked for special rocks under the water—the ones that are beautiful until you take them out of the water, when they get dry and not so bright.

We found skipping stones and tried to see who could get the most skips from a stone.

We saw a school of minnows going as fast as they could to get away from us.

But we didn't see any frogs.

"If you want to see frogs," my father said, "you'll have to walk down the bank a ways and look hard."

So we decided to do that.

"Fine!" my father said. "But I'll stay here. I think I'm ready for a little nap."

"Naps are boring!" we said.

"Sometimes it's nice to be bored," my father said.

We left him with his eyes closed, sitting under a tree.

Huey saw the first frog. He almost stepped on it. It jumped into the water, and we ran after it.

Huey caught it and picked it up, and then I saw another one. I grabbed it.

It was slippery and strong and its body was cold, just like it wasn't the middle of summer.

Then Gloria caught one too. The frogs wriggled in our hands, and we felt their hearts beating. Huey looked at their funny webbed feet.

"Their feet are good for swimming," he said, "but Dad is wrong. They don't wear shoes!"

"No way," Gloria said. "They sure don't wear shoes."

"Let's go tell him," I said.

We threw our frogs back into the river. They made little trails swimming away from us. And then we went back to my father.

He was sitting under the tree with his eyes shut. It looked like he hadn't moved an inch.

"We found frogs," Huey said, "and we've got news for you. They don't wear shoes!"

My father's eyes opened. "They don't?" he said. "Well, I can't be right about everything. Dry your feet. Put your shoes on. It's time to go."

We all sat down to put on our shoes.

I pulled out a sock and put it on.

I stuck my foot into my shoe. My foot wouldn't go in.

I picked up the shoe and looked inside.

"Oh no!" I yelled.

There were two little eyes inside my shoe, looking out at me. Huey and Gloria grabbed their socks. All our shoes had frogs in them, every one.

"What did I tell you," my father said.

"You were right," we said. "It's a day when frogs wear shoes!"

The Soup Stone

*a Belgian folk tale
retold by
Maria Leach*

One day a soldier was walking home from the wars and came to a village. The wind was cold; the sky was gray, and the soldier was hungry. He stopped at a house on the edge of the village and asked for something to eat. "We have nothing for ourselves," the people said, so the soldier went on.

He stopped at the next house and asked for something to eat. "We have nothing ourselves," the people said.

"Have you got a big pot?" the soldier said. Yes, they had a big iron pot.

"Have you got water?" he asked. Yes, they had plenty of water.

"Fill the pot with water and put it on the fire," the soldier said, "for I have a soup stone with me."

"A soup stone?" they asked. "What is that?"

"It is a stone that makes soup," the soldier replied. And they all gathered round to see this wonder.

The woman of the house filled the big pot with water and hung it over the fire. The soldier took a stone from his pocket (it looked like any stone a man might pick up on the road) and tossed it into the pot. "Now let it boil," he said. So they all sat down to wait for the pot to boil.

"Could you spare a bit of salt for it?" the soldier asked.

"Of course," the woman said, and she pulled out the salt box. The soldier took a fistful of salt and threw it in, for it was a big pot. Then they all sat back to wait.

"A few carrots would taste good in it," the soldier said longingly.

"Oh, we have a few carrots," the woman said, and she pulled them out from under a bench, where the soldier had been eying them. So they threw in the carrots. And while the carrots boiled, the soldier told them stories of his adventures.

"A few potatoes would be good, wouldn't they?" the soldier said. "They'd thicken the soup a bit."

"We have a few potatoes," said the oldest girl. "I'll get them." So they put the potatoes in the pot and waited for the soup to boil.

"An onion does give a good flavor," the soldier said.

"Run next door and ask the neighbor for an onion," the farmer told his smallest son. The child ran out of the house and came back with three onions. So they put the onions in. While they were waiting, they were cracking jokes and telling tales.

"... And I haven't tasted cabbage since I left my mother's house," the soldier was saying.

"Run out in the garden and pull a cabbage," said the mother. And a small girl ran out and came back with a cabbage. And they put that in.

"It won't be long now," the soldier said.

"Just a little longer," the woman said, stirring the pot with a long ladle.

At that moment the oldest son came in. He had been hunting and brought home two rabbits.

"Just what we need for the finishing touch!" cried the soldier, and it was only a matter of minutes before the rabbits were cut up and thrown into the pot.

"Ha!" said the hungry hunter. "The smell of a fine soup."

"The traveler has brought a soup stone," the farmer said to his son, "and he is making soup with it in the pot."

At last the soup was ready, and it was good. There was enough for all: the soldier and the farmer and his wife, the oldest girl and the oldest son, the little girl, and the little son.

"It's a wonderful soup," the farmer said.

"It's a wonderful stone," the wife said.

"It is," the soldier said, "and it will make soup forever if you follow the formula we used today."

So they finished the soup. And when the soldier said good-bye, he gave the woman the stone to pay back the kindness. She protested politely.

"It's nothing," the soldier said and went on his way without the stone.

Luckily, he found another just before he came to the next village.

The City Mouse and the Country Mouse

a fable by Aesop

There was once a happy little Country Mouse, who lived in a big wheat field. In the summer she feasted on grains of wheat or on bits of bread from the farmers' lunch boxes. When the weather grew cold she moved into the farmhouse and picked up bits of cake and bread and cheese which the cook dropped on the kitchen floor. These she stored away in her little mouse hole in the attic until she had a good supply laid in for the winter.

Now one day during the winter the little Country Mouse's cousin, a City Mouse, came to visit her. When they had chatted for a while, the little Country Mouse took her visitor to see her attic pantry. Proudly she showed her the mound of cheese bits, the heaps of bread and cake crumbs, and the neat piles of nuts and dried peas.

But when the City Mouse had eaten a hearty dinner, she wiped her whiskers daintily and said, "You poor thing! So this is the way you live, on left-overs dried up in the attic. Come with me to the city and I will show you a real feast!"

The Country Mouse immediately felt rather ashamed of her simple home, so she quietly went along with the City Mouse to visit her.

The City Mouse led the way into a huge brick house, up a great staircase, and into a dining room.

The rich people who lived in the big house with the City Mouse were just having dinner, so the two little mice hid behind the door.

"Keep very still," said the City Mouse. "When they leave the table we can have all the food that is left."

The eyes of the little Country Mouse grew big and round at that, for she had never seen so much food in her whole busy life. So she sat very still until, with a scuffling of feet and scraping of chairs, the big people left the table.

"Come on," squeaked the City Mouse. Peeking cautiously to right and left she led the way across the room, up onto a chair, and from the chair onto the table, with the Country Mouse scampering along behind her.

The Country Mouse took a long look around her at the table still crowded with good things, and sighed a deep, happy sigh.

"This is wonderful," she said, taking a big bite out of a beautiful cheese. "You live just like a prince!"

She had scarcely finished squeaking when, with a snarl, a cat pounced up on the table. After her came the cook, shouting and waving a big spoon. And into the room bounded two dogs, barking fiercely. Then there was a terrible row! In the midst of it the two mice skittered down to the floor and dodged into a handy hole.

"We'll wait until all is quiet again and go back for some more," whispered the City Mouse.

But her country cousin shook her head firmly.

"We'll wait until it is quiet again and then I'll go home as fast as I can. You are welcome to all the fine food you can get, my friend. As for me, I prefer my dry crusts in my peaceful attic!"

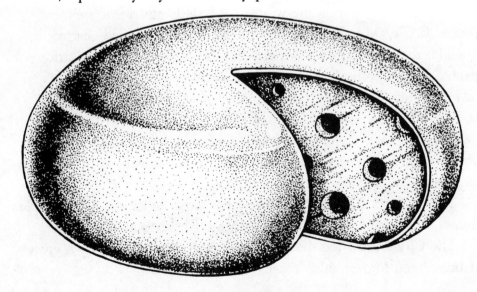

How the Stars Came to Be

a story adapted from several Native American tales
by Lynn Moroney

Long, long ago there were no stars in the sky. In the day there was the sun, and at night there was the moon, but there was not one star in the sky. On some nights Moon gave a bright light, but some nights Moon gave only part of her light, and on some nights . . . Moon gave no light at all. On those nights it was always so dark that the animals were frightened. So once, when it was especially dark, the animals decided to ask Great Spirit for help.

Great Spirit listened to all the animals and then said, "You shall have light, but this is what you must do. Go to the river, and gather all the small stones you can carry. Do not gather the stones that are big and round and smooth like Sun and Moon. Return with only those stones that are small and have sharp, pointed edges."

The animals did not understand this, but they did as they were told. They all hurried to the river, gathered all the small, pointed stones they could carry, and returned to the Great Spirit.

Then, in the still of the night, while the animals looked on, Great Spirit took one of the small stones and carefully placed it high in the sky. At once the little stone began to sparkle and twinkle and dance. Great Spirit said, "That will be called a STAR." And, oh, the animals thought it a lovely sight (no one had ever seen a star before).

Great Spirit then took more stones and began to place them in just such a way that they made a picture. . . . a star picture! It was a picture of Fisher! The animals loved Fisher, and they were pleased to see his picture in the sky.

Then Great Spirit told the animals, "Now you may go into the sky and make your own pictures with the stones you gathered. You must return before morning, and should you need more stones to finish your pictures, call for Coyote; he will carry extra stones." Great Spirit then handed Coyote a big sack. It was filled with many stones.

One by one, the animals began going up into the sky. Crow went to one place, Swan went to another, Eagle to another, Bear to yet another. Soon the sky was filled with animals—all busily making pictures.

Coyote stood around looking at the sack. He did not want to be bothered with helping the animals. Finally, he began to walk up into the sky. He dragged the sack along, saying that if some animals could not carry very many stones, that was their misfortune.

Coyote went along thinking to himself, "This sack is too heavy. There are too many stones for me to carry." Coyote reached down into that sack, he took some of those little stones, and he threw them way high into the sky. They stuck at the top and they began to flash and twinkle and sparkle. The stones had turned to stars!

Coyote walked on a little further. Again, he began to complain. He moaned that he didn't want to carry those extra stones. He said that he was going to be busy making his own picture. Again, he reached into the sack and threw away more stones. Coyote kept doing this . . . walking along . . . throwing away stones, walking along . . . scattering stones, walking along . . . tossing stones.

Now when Little Dog, who was just a puppy, finally got to the top of the sky, he had just two stones—not enough to make a good picture. Needing more stones, he began to call, "Coyote! Co-yo-te! Where are you?"

Coyote was nowhere to be found.

By this time, even the big animals had run out of stones, and they began to call, "Coyote! Co-yo-te! Where are you?"

Coyote was nowhere to be found.

Just then, Rooster called out, "Er-Er-Er-er-oo-oo-ooo! Morning is coming! Morning is coming!" (Rooster knew about these things.) The night was almost over, and some of the animals were not finished! The animals began to run around, looking here and there and calling, "Coyote, Coyote!"

At last someone called out, "Here he is! Here is Coyote!" And there was Coyote. He was sound asleep, and right next to him was an EMPTY SACK!

Nothing could be done.

The animals had to return to Earth. Some of them never finished their pictures.

And this is why, on clear nights, if we look up at the stars, we can see pictures, and why some of the pictures look like they are not quite "finished," and why some stars don't make pictures at all. Those are the stars Coyote carelessly threw away. And though many of the animals were unable to finish their pictures, they were never again frightened by the dark night, for since that time, the night has been filled with the soft light of many stars.

But when Coyote threw away all those stones, he forgot to do one important thing...Yes!...Coyote forgot to make his own picture!

And that is why to this very night, when Coyote looks up and sees all those wasted stars, he remembers how foolish he was, and knowing he can't blame anyone but himself, he begins to howl, "OW-OO-OO-OO-oo-oooo!"

And now you know how the stars came to be, and now you know why Coyote howls. And now this story is finished, and if you like it, remember to tell it to someone...for that is the way of stories!

IT COULD ALWAYS BE WORSE

a Yiddish folk tale
retold by Margot Zemach

Once upon a time in a small village a poor unfortunate man lived with his mother, his wife, and his six children in a little one-room hut. Because they were so crowded, the man and his wife often argued. The children were noisy, and they fought. In winter, when the nights were long and the days were cold, life was especially hard. The hut was full of crying and quarreling. One day, when the poor unfortunate man couldn't stand it any more, he ran to the Rabbi for advice.

"Holy Rabbi," he cried, "things are in a bad way with me, and getting worse. We are so poor that my mother, my wife, my six children, and I all live together in one small hut. We are too crowded, and there's so much noise. Help me, Rabbi. I'll do whatever you say."

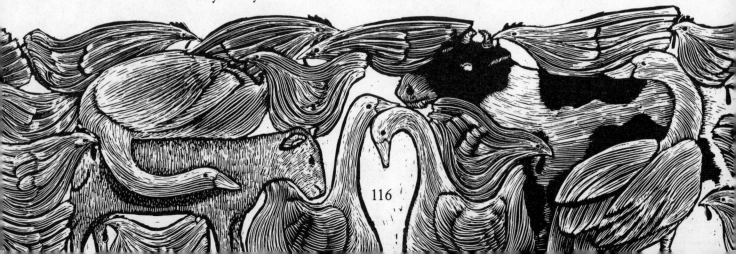

The Rabbi thought and pulled on his beard. At last he said, "Tell me, my poor man, do you have any animals, perhaps a chicken or two?"

"Yes," said the man. "I do have a few chickens, also a rooster and a goose."

"Ah, fine," said the Rabbi. "Now go home and take the chickens, the rooster, and the goose into your hut to live with you."

"Yes indeed, Rabbi," said the man, though he was a bit surprised.

The poor unfortunate man hurried home and took the chickens, the rooster, and the goose out of the shed and into his little hut.

When some days or a week had gone by, life in the hut was worse than before. Now with the quarreling and crying there was honking, crowing, and clucking. There were feathers in the soup. The hut stayed just as small and the children grew bigger. When the poor unfortunate man couldn't stand it any longer, he again ran to the Rabbi for help.

"Holy Rabbi," he cried, "see what a misfortune has befallen me. Now with the crying and quarreling, with the honking, clucking, and crowing, there are feathers in the soup. Rabbi, it couldn't be worse. Help me, please."

The Rabbi listened and thought. At last he said, "Tell me, do you happen to have a goat?"

"Oh, yes, I do have an old goat, but he's not worth much."

"Excellent," said the Rabbi. "Now go home and take the old goat into your hut to live with you."

"Ah, no! Do you really mean it, Rabbi?" cried the man.

"Come, come now, my good man, and do as I say at once," said the Rabbi.

The poor unfortunate man tramped back home with his head hanging down and took the old goat into his hut.

When some days or a week had gone by, life in the little hut was much worse. Now, with the crying, quarreling, clucking, honking, and crowing, the goat went wild, pushing and butting everyone with his horns. The hut seemed smaller, the children grew bigger.

117

When the poor unfortunate man couldn't stand it another minute, he again ran to the Rabbi.

"Holy Rabbi, help me!" he screamed. "Now the goat is running wild. My life is a nightmare."

The Rabbi listened and thought. At last he said, "Tell me, my poor man. Is it possible that you have a cow? Young or old doesn't matter."

"Yes, Rabbi, it's true I have a cow," said the poor man fearfully.

"Go home then," said the Rabbi, "and take the cow into your hut."

"Oh, no, surely not, Rabbi!" cried the man.

"Do it at once," said the Rabbi.

The poor unfortunate man trudged home with a heavy heart and took the cow into his hut. Is the Rabbi crazy? he thought.

When some days or a week had gone by, life in the hut was very much worse than before. Everyone quarreled, even the chickens. The goat ran wild. The cow trampled everything. The poor man could hardly believe his misfortune. At last, when he could stand it no longer, he ran to the Rabbi for help.

"Holy Rabbi," he shrieked, "help me, save me, the end of the world has come! The cow is trampling everything. There is no room even to breathe. It's worse than a nightmare!"

The Rabbi listened and thought. At last he said, "Go home now, my poor unfortunate man, and let the animals out of your hut."

"I will, I will, I'll do it right away," said the man.

The poor unfortunate man hurried home and let the cow, the goat, the chickens, the goose, and the rooster out of his little hut.

That night the poor man and all his family slept peacefully. There was no crowing, no clucking, no honking. There was plenty of room to breathe.

The very next day the poor man ran back to the Rabbi.

"Holy Rabbi," he cried, "you have made life sweet for me. With just my family in the hut, it's so quiet, so roomy, so peaceful . . . What a pleasure!"

EEYORE HAS A BIRTHDAY AND GETS TWO PRESENTS

from Winnie-the-Pooh *by A. A. Milne*

Eeyore, the old grey Donkey, stood by the side of the stream, and looked at himself in the water.

"Pathetic," he said. "That's what it is. Pathetic."

He turned and walked slowly down the stream for twenty yards, splashed across it, and walked slowly back on the other side. Then he looked at himself in the water again.

"As I thought," he said. "No better from *this* side. But nobody minds. Nobody cares. Pathetic, that's what it is."

There was a crackling noise in the bracken behind him, and out came Pooh.

"Good morning, Eeyore," said Pooh.

"Good morning, Pooh Bear," said Eeyore gloomily. "If it *is* a good morning," he said. "Which I doubt," said he.

"Why, what's the matter?"

"Nothing, Pooh Bear, nothing. We can't all, and some of us don't. That's all there is to it."

"Can't all *what?*" said Pooh, rubbing his nose.

"Gaiety. Song-and-dance. Here we go round the mulberry bush."

"Oh!" said Pooh. He thought for a long time, and then asked, "What mulberry bush is that?"

"Bon-hommy," went on Eeyore gloomily. "French word meaning bonhommy," he explained. "I'm not complaining, but There It Is."

Pooh sat down on a large stone, and tried to think this out. It sounded to him like a riddle, and he was never much good at riddles, being a Bear of Very Little Brain. So he sang *Cottleston Pie* instead:

Cottleston, Cottleston, Cottleston Pie,
A fly can't bird, but a bird can fly.
Ask me a riddle and I reply:
"Cottleston, Cottleston, Cottleston Pie."

That was the first verse. When he had finished it, Eeyore didn't actually say that he didn't like it, so Pooh very kindly sang the second verse to him:

Cottleston, Cottleston, Cottleston Pie,
A fish can't whistle and neither can I.
Ask me a riddle and I reply:
"Cottleston, Cottleston, Cottleston Pie."

Eeyore still said nothing at all, so Pooh hummed the third verse quietly to himself:

Cottleston, Cottleston, Cottleston Pie,
Why does a chicken, I don't know why.
Ask me a riddle and I reply:
"Cottleston, Cottleston, Cottleston Pie."

"That's right," said Eeyore. "Sing. Umty-tiddly, umty-too. Here we go gathering Nuts and May. Enjoy yourself."

"I am," said Pooh.

"Some can," said Eeyore.

"Why, what's the matter?"

"*Is* anything the matter?"

"You seem so sad, Eeyore."

"Sad? Why should I be sad? It's my birthday. The happiest day of the year."

"Your birthday?" said Pooh in great surprise.

"Of course it is. Can't you see? Look at all the presents I have had." He waved a foot from side to side. "Look at the birthday cake. Candles and pink sugar."

Pooh looked—first to the right and then to the left.

"Presents?" said Pooh. "Birthday cake?" said Pooh. *"Where?"*

"Can't you see them?"

"No," said Pooh.

"Neither can I," said Eeyore. "Joke," he explained. "Ha ha!"

Pooh scratched his head, being a little puzzled by all this.

"But is it really your birthday?" he asked.

"It is."

"Oh! Well, Many happy returns of the day, Eeyore."

"And many happy returns to you, Pooh Bear."

"But it isn't *my* birthday."

"No, it's mine."

"But you said 'Many happy returns'—"

"Well, why not? You don't always want to be miserable on my birthday, do you?"

"Oh, I see," said Pooh.

"It's bad enough," said Eeyore, almost breaking down, "being miserable myself, what with no presents and no cake and no candles, and no proper notice taken of me at all, but if everybody else is going to be miserable too—"

This was too much for Pooh. "Stay there!" he called to Eeyore, as he turned and hurried back home as quick as he could; for he felt that he must get poor Eeyore a present of *some* sort at once, and he could always think of a proper one afterwards.

Outside his house he found Piglet, jumping up and down trying to reach the knocker.

"Hallo, Piglet," he said.

"Hallo, Pooh," said Piglet.

"What are *you* trying to do?"

"I was trying to reach the knocker," said Piglet. "I just came round—"

"Let me do it for you," said Pooh kindly. So he reached up and knocked at the door. "I have just seen Eeyore," he began, "and poor Eeyore is in a Very Sad Condition, because it's his birthday, and nobody has taken any notice of it, and he's very Gloomy—you know what Eeyore is—and there he was, and— What a long time whoever lives here is answering this door." And he knocked again.

"But Pooh," said Piglet, "it's your own house!"

"Oh!" said Pooh. "So it is," he said. "Well, let's go in."

So in they went. The first thing Pooh did was to go to the cupboard to see if he had quite a small jar of honey left; and he had, so he took it down.

"I'm giving this to Eeyore," he explained, "as a present. What are *you* going to give?"

"Couldn't I give it too?" said Piglet. "From both of us?"

"No," said Pooh. "That would *not* be a good plan."

"All right, then, I'll give him a balloon. I've got one left from my party. I'll go and get it now, shall I?"

"That, Piglet, is a *very* good idea. It is just what Eeyore wants to cheer him up. Nobody can be uncheered with a balloon."

So off Piglet trotted; and in the other direction went Pooh, with his jar of honey.

It was a warm day, and he had a long way to go. He hadn't gone more than halfway when a sort of funny feeling began to creep all over him. It began at the tip of his nose and trickled all through him and out at the soles of his feet. It was just as if somebody inside him were saying, "Now then, Pooh, time for a little something."

"Dear, dear," said Pooh, "I didn't know it was as late as that." So he sat down and took the top off his jar of honey. "Lucky I brought this with me," he thought. "Many a bear going out on a warm day like this would never have thought of bringing a little something with him." And he began to eat.

"Now let me see," he thought, as he took his last lick of the inside of the jar, "where was I going? Ah, yes, Eeyore." He got up slowly.

And then, suddenly, he remembered. He had eaten Eeyore's birthday present!

"Bother!" said Pooh. "What *shall* I do? I *must* give him *something.*"

For a little while he couldn't think of anything. Then he thought: "Well, it's a very nice pot, even if there's no honey in it, and if I washed it clean, and got somebody to write 'A Happy Birthday' on it, Eeyore could keep things in it, which might be Useful." So, as he was just passing the Hundred Acre Wood, he went inside to call on Owl, who lived there.

"Good morning, Owl," he said.

"Good morning, Pooh," said Owl.

"Many happy returns of Eeyore's birthday," said Pooh.

"Oh, is that what it is?"

"What are you giving him, Owl?"

"What are *you* giving him, Pooh?"

"I'm giving him a Useful Pot to Keep Things In, and I wanted to ask you—"

"Is this it?" said Owl, taking it out of Pooh's paw.

"Yes, and I wanted to ask you—"

"Somebody has been keeping honey in it," said Owl.

"You can keep *anything* in it," said Pooh earnestly. "It's Very Useful like that. And I wanted to ask you—"

"You ought to write 'A Happy Birthday' on it."

"*That* was what I wanted to ask you," said Pooh. "Because my spelling is Wobbly. It's good spelling but it Wobbles, and the letters get in the wrong places. Would *you* write 'A Happy Birthday' on it for me?"

"It's a nice pot," said Owl, looking at it all round. "Couldn't I give it too? From both of us?"

"No," said Pooh. "That would *not* be a good plan. Now I'll just wash it first, and then you can write on it."

Well, he washed the pot out, and dried it, while Owl licked the end of his pencil, and wondered how to spell "birthday."

"Can you read, Pooh?" he asked, a little anxiously. "There's a notice about knocking and ringing outside my door, which Christopher Robin wrote. Could you read it?"

"Christopher Robin told me what it said, and *then* I could."

"Well, I'll tell you what *this* says, and then you'll be able to."

So Owl wrote . . . and this is what he wrote:

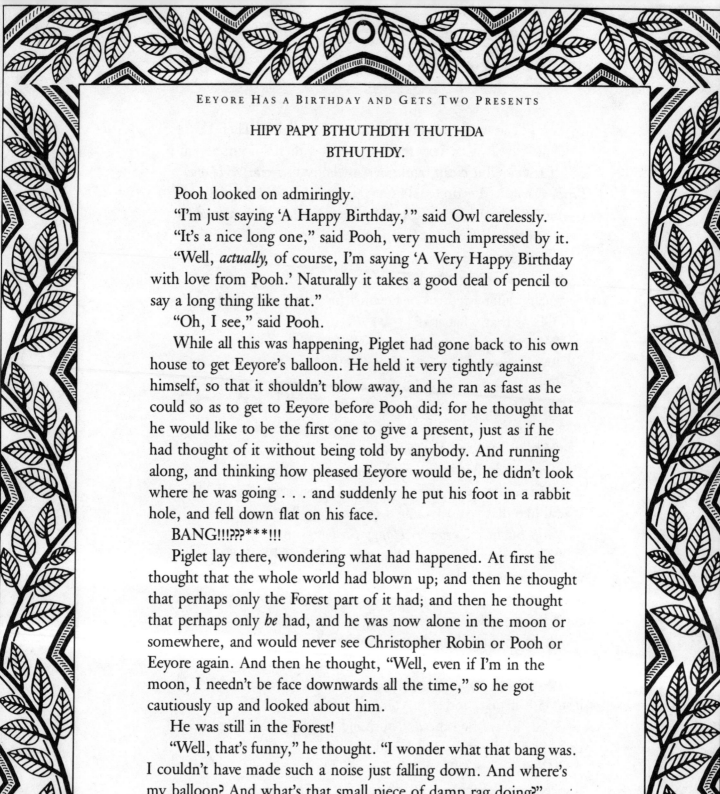

HIPY PAPY BTHUTHDTH THUTHDA
BTHUTHDY.

Pooh looked on admiringly.

"I'm just saying 'A Happy Birthday,'" said Owl carelessly.

"It's a nice long one," said Pooh, very much impressed by it.

"Well, *actually*, of course, I'm saying 'A Very Happy Birthday with love from Pooh.' Naturally it takes a good deal of pencil to say a long thing like that."

"Oh, I see," said Pooh.

While all this was happening, Piglet had gone back to his own house to get Eeyore's balloon. He held it very tightly against himself, so that it shouldn't blow away, and he ran as fast as he could so as to get to Eeyore before Pooh did; for he thought that he would like to be the first one to give a present, just as if he had thought of it without being told by anybody. And running along, and thinking how pleased Eeyore would be, he didn't look where he was going . . . and suddenly he put his foot in a rabbit hole, and fell down flat on his face.

BANG!!!???***!!!

Piglet lay there, wondering what had happened. At first he thought that the whole world had blown up; and then he thought that perhaps only the Forest part of it had; and then he thought that perhaps only *he* had, and he was now alone in the moon or somewhere, and would never see Christopher Robin or Pooh or Eeyore again. And then he thought, "Well, even if I'm in the moon, I needn't be face downwards all the time," so he got cautiously up and looked about him.

He was still in the Forest!

"Well, that's funny," he thought. "I wonder what that bang was. I couldn't have made such a noise just falling down. And where's my balloon? And what's that small piece of damp rag doing?"

It was the balloon!

"Oh, dear!" said Piglet. "Oh dear, oh, dearie, dearie, dear! Well, it's too late now. I can't go back, and I haven't another balloon, and perhaps Eeyore doesn't *like* balloons so *very* much."

So he trotted on, rather sadly now, and down he came to the side of the stream where Eeyore was, and called out to him.

"Good morning, Eeyore," shouted Piglet.

"Good morning, Little Piglet," said Eeyore. "If it *is* a good morning," he said. "Which I doubt," said he. "Not that it matters," he said.

"Many happy returns of the day," said Piglet, having now got closer.

Eeyore stopped looking at himself in the stream, and turned to stare at Piglet.

"Just say that again," he said.

"Many hap—"

"Wait a moment."

Balancing on three legs, he began to bring his fourth leg very cautiously up to his ear. "I did this yesterday," he explained, as he fell down for the third time. "It's quite easy. It's so as I can hear better. . . . There, that's done it! Now then, what were you saying?" He pushed his ear forward with his hoof.

"Many happy returns of the day," said Piglet again.

"Meaning me?"

"Of course, Eeyore."

"My birthday?"

"Yes."

"Me having a real birthday?"

"Yes, Eeyore, and I've brought you a present."

Eeyore took down his right hoof from his right ear, turned round, and with great difficulty put up his left hoof.

"I must have that in the other ear," he said. "Now then."

"A present," said Piglet very loudly.

"Meaning me again?"

"Yes."

"My birthday still?"

"Of course, Eeyore."

"Me going on having a real birthday?"

"Yes, Eeyore, and I brought you a balloon."

"*Balloon?*" said Eeyore. "You did say balloon? One of those big coloured things you blow up? Gaiety, song-and-dance, here we are and there we are?"

"Yes, but I'm afraid—I'm very sorry, Eeyore—but when I was running along to bring it to you, I fell down."

"Dear, dear, how unlucky! You ran too fast, I expect. You didn't hurt yourself, Little Piglet?"

"No, but I—I—oh, Eeyore, I burst the balloon!"

There was a very long silence.

"My balloon?" said Eeyore at last.

Piglet nodded.

"My birthday balloon?"

"Yes, Eeyore," said Piglet sniffing a little. "Here it is. With—with many happy returns of the day." And he gave Eeyore the small piece of damp rag.

"Is this it?" said Eeyore, a little surprised.

Piglet nodded.

"My present?"

Piglet nodded again.

"The balloon?"

"Yes."

"Thank you, Piglet," said Eeyore. "You don't mind my asking," he went on, "but what colour was this balloon when it—when it *was* a balloon?"

"Red."

"I just wondered. . . . Red," he murmured to himself. "My favourite colour. . . . How big was it?"

"About as big as me."

"I just wondered. . . . About as big as Piglet," he said to himself sadly. "My favourite size. Well, well."

Piglet felt very miserable, and didn't know what to say. He was still opening his mouth to begin something, and then deciding that it wasn't any good saying *that*, when he heard a shout from the other side of the river, and there was Pooh.

"Many happy returns of the day," called out Pooh, forgetting that he had said it already.

"Thank you, Pooh, I'm having them," said Eeyore gloomily.

"I've brought you a little present," said Pooh excitedly.

"I've had it," said Eeyore.

Pooh had now splashed across the stream to Eeyore, and Piglet was sitting a little way off, his head in his paws, snuffling to himself.

"It's a Useful Pot," said Pooh. "Here it is. And it's got 'A Very Happy Birthday with love from Pooh' written on it. That's what all that writing is. And it's for putting things in. There!"

When Eeyore saw the pot, he became quite excited.

"Why!" he said. "I believe my Balloon will just go into that Pot!"

"Oh, no, Eeyore," said Pooh. "Balloons are much too big to go into Pots. What you do with a balloon is, you hold the balloon—"

"Not mine," said Eeyore proudly. "Look, Piglet!" And as Piglet looked sorrowfully round, Eeyore picked the balloon up with his teeth, and placed it carefully in the pot; picked it out and put it on the ground; and then picked it up again and put it carefully back.

"So it does!" said Pooh. "It goes in!"

"So it does!" said Piglet. "And it comes out!"

"Doesn't it?" said Eeyore. "It goes in and out like anything."

"I'm very glad," said Pooh happily, "that I thought of giving you a Useful Pot to put things in."

"I'm very glad," said Piglet happily, "that I thought of giving you Something to put in a Useful Pot."

But Eeyore wasn't listening. He was taking the balloon out, and putting it back again, as happy as could be.

A House with a Star Inside

a story retold by Melissa Heckler

Once upon a time there was a little boy. Oh, he was maybe six or seven years old. One day he went to his mother and he said, "I'm bored."

His mother looked at him and he looked at her, and she said with a twinkle in her eye, "You go outside and see if you can find me a little red, round house with no windows and no doors, a chimney on top, and a star inside."

The boy thought about that. Houses weren't round. A round, red house with no windows, no doors, a chimney on top, and a star inside? Well, he was out the door quickly. He looked around his neighborhood,

128

but all he saw were square houses and houses with windows and doors. He saw lots of chimneys, but he saw no stars, at least not from the outside, so he went on down the road. He was walking and walking, and he saw a girl. He said to her, "Have you seen a red, round house with no windows, no doors, a chimney on top, and a star inside?"

The girl thought for a minute and then she said, "No, I haven't seen a house like that anywhere. I've seen square houses, and I've seen long houses, and I've seen thin houses, but I've never seen a red, round house. But, you know, my father's a farmer, and maybe he'll know 'cause he's seen lots of things."

So the girl and the boy walked on back to her father's farm, and they walked on into the barn where her father was standing. He paused when he saw the two children. They went right up to him and the little girl said, "Papa, this little boy needs some help."

The boy asked the farmer, "Have you seen a red, round house with no windows, no doors, a chimney on top, and a star inside?"

The farmer said, "Hmmmm. I've seen red barns. I've seen all kinds of differently shaped houses. In fact, I've even seen round barns, but I've never seen a red, round house with no windows, no doors, a chimney on top, and a star inside. But I have an idea. You go on down the road and ask Granny. Granny's likely to be sitting out on her front porch rocking. She's old and she's seen lots of things in her time. Maybe she'll have seen one."

So the boy thanked the farmer and the girl, and he ran on down the road till he came to Granny's house. He opened the gate and he went up the front steps. He stopped right on Granny's front porch. "Granny!" he said.

"Good morning," said Granny. "Good morning," said the boy. "Granny, Granny, I'm looking for a red, round house with no windows, no doors, a chimney on top, and a star inside. Have you ever seen one like that?"

Granny rocked and rocked and rocked, then she said, "I've seen lots of things in my day. I've seen lots of kinds of houses, but I've never seen a red, round house with no windows, no doors, a chimney on top, and a star inside. But I'd sure like to read of an evening in a house with a star inside, so if you find that house, you come back and tell me." Granny rocked some more. "Now I have an idea," she said. "You go out into the road and you go ask the wind, because the wind has seen everything and been everywhere. I think perhaps the wind will tell you."

So the boy thanked Granny. He ran down the steps, ran back out the gate, and he just stood in the middle of the road. He opened his arms wide and he shouted, "WIND! WIND! HAVE YOU SEEN A RED, ROUND HOUSE WITH NO WINDOWS, NO DOORS, A CHIMNEY ON TOP, AND A STAR INSIDE?"

Then he waited. Pretty soon he felt a little push at his back. Just a little breeze, it was. But as he waited, the breeze picked up. It was just a little wind, but it seemed to be pushing the boy down the road. So he just went on, feeling the wind at his back, and it pushed him right up a hill. When he got to the top of that hill, the wind pushed him just a little further, until he was standing right beneath a tree. He looked up at the tree. He saw its leaves. Through the leaves he saw one other thing. It was an apple. Just then, the wind came, and it blew that apple right off the tree so it fell down at the boy's feet. The boy picked up the apple, and he looked at it. It was red and round. It had no windows, no doors, and a chimney on top. But where was the star?

The boy didn't wait more than ten seconds. He ran off down the road. He ran past Granny's house and he yelled, "Granny, I think I've found it! I'll come back and show you!"

He ran on to his mother. He ran through the front door of his house and he called, "Mama! Mama! I think I've found it!"

His mother came. When she saw he had an apple, she got out a knife and sat down at the kitchen table. She lay the apple on its side and carefully cut it in half. There, right in the center of each half, was a beautiful five-pointed star!

Well, the boy did go back to Granny, and he went back to the farmer and to the girl, too. He showed them all what he had found: a red, round house with no windows, no doors, a chimney on top, and a star inside.

THE TALE OF THE TALES

a Russian folk tale
by George and Helen Papashvily

There was, there was, and yet there was not, there was once a boy who lived far away in time and in place from where you read these words.

This boy's greatest delight was to hear the stories the men of his village told every night as they gathered around a campfire.

From the minute the flames flared high until the last coals shut their red eyes and fell asleep in their soft black blankets spun from soot, the boy listened while the men, in turn, each told a tale.

Then one night as the stories were going around, the oldest man turned to the boy and said, "Now it's your turn to tell one."

131

"I cannot," the boy said. "I do not know how to begin."

"That is easy," the old man answered. "For stories always begin the same way—There was, there was, and yet there was not—. It means that what comes after is true and true but then again not so true. Or perhaps it means that what is true for two men is not true for three."

"I will try," the boy said. "There was, there was and yet there—. No. I can't tell a story. I can't even read."

"So much the better," the old man told him. "Neither can I. Those who read have stories of their own they keep locked up in books. We have ours and they are better for they live with us day by day in our hearts."

"But I am afraid I might not remember every word of the story exactly right."

"What difference does that make? No two people ever tell any story the same way. Why should they? A story is a letter that comes to us from yesterday. Each man who tells it adds his word to the message and sends it on to tomorrow. So begin."

"Well," the boy said, "there was, there was and—" He looked around the circle and saw all the eyes watching him and the rest of the words turned to pebbles in his mouth and he stopped.

"Go on," the old man said, "go on, or you have no right to listen any more. To listen to stories without ever telling one is harvesting grain without sowing seeds; it is picking fruit without pruning the tree."

When he heard this, the boy knew he could hesitate no longer and so he began:

MARGARET H. LIPPERT is a professional storyteller who comes from a family of Irish storytellers. A classroom teacher for many years, she taught children's literature and storytelling at Bank Street College of Education and at Teacher's College, Columbia University, where she earned her doctorate. She has lived and taught in Tanzania, East Africa, and in Guatemala, Central America. She now lives in the Cascade Mountains in Washington State with her husband and two daughters.

Authors and Storytellers

Aesop (620-560 B.C.?), author of "The City Mouse and the Country Mouse," was a Greek slave. For many years, Aesop's fables were handed down orally from generation to generation. No one knows how many of the stories attributed to Aesop were actually composed by him.

Andersen, Hans Christian (1805-1875), author of "The Emperor's New Clothes," was a Danish writer of fairy tales. His stories, with their sly humor, wisdom, and simplicity, can be considered both children's and adult's literature.

Babbitt, Ellen C., reteller of "The Foolish, Timid Rabbit," retold many animal stories from India in her book *Jataka Tales*.

Baylor, Byrd, collected the stories "How Our People Came to Be" and "Why Saguaros Grow on the South Side of Hills." Baylor grew up in the deserts of America's Southwest and spent many childhood summers in Mexico. This experience resulted in a variety of books for children, including *Before You Came This Way*. Baylor received the Caldecott Medal from the American Library Association in 1973 for *When Clay Sings*, and again in 1976 for *The Desert Is Theirs*. She resides in Arizona and New Mexico.

Bryan, Ashley, teller of "Hen and Frog," was born in New York City. His parents came from the island of Antigua. He was formerly a professor at Dartmouth College. Bryan now has a studio on Little Cranberry Island in Maine. He has written, compiled, and illustrated many books, including *The Ox of the Wonderful Horns and Other African Folktales; Beat the Story Drum, Pum-Pum;* and *The Cat's Purr*.

Cameron, Ann, author of "A Day When Frogs Wear Shoes," was born in Wisconsin. She now lives in Guatemala and New York City. Her recent books include *More Stories Julian Tells* and *Julian, Secret Agent*.

Credle, Ellis, teller of "A Tall Turnip," collected many stories of Appalachia in his book *Tall Tales from the High Hills*.

Ehrlich, Amy, teller of "The Emperor's New Clothes" and "The Elves and the Shoemaker," has adapted many fairy tales, some of which can be found in her book *The Random House Book of Fairy Tales*.

Erdoes, Richard, and Ortiz, Alfonso, retellers of "Turkey Makes the Corn and Coyote Plants It," based their version of this myth on Grenville Goodwin's retelling in *Myths and Tales of the White Mountain Apache* [1939].

Grimm, Jacob (1785-1863) and his brother Wilhelm (1786-1859), tellers of "The Elves and the Shoemaker" and "Little Red Riding Hood," were German philologists and folklorists.

Hamilton, Virginia, teller of "A Wolf and Little Daughter," is a recipient of the Coretta Scott King Award and the National Book Award. *The People Could Fly*, from which this selection was taken, draws upon her lifelong interest in folklore.

Hatch, Mary C., reteller of "The Wonderful Knapsack," is also the author of *13 Danish Tales*.

Haviland, Virginia, reteller of "Jack and the Beanstalk," is a well-known and highly acclaimed expert in the field of children's literature. She served as the Reading Advisor for Children at the Boston Public Library, and for nearly twenty years was the Head of the Children's Book Section of the Library of Congress. She was also a chairperson of the Newbery-Caldecott Awards Committee, a judge for the National Book Award in children's literature, and a jury member for the Hans Christian Andersen Medal. In 1976, Haviland received the Regina Medal for distinguished service in the field of children's literature.

Hayes, Joe, reteller of "La Hormiguita," has based many of his stories on tales from the varied cultures of New Mexico. His books of stories include *The Day It Snowed Tortillas* and *The Checker-Playing Hound Dog*.

Hearn, Lafcadio (1850-1904), reteller of "The Old Woman Who Lost Her Dumplings," wrote many fantastic tales set in the West Indies and Japan. Hearn was born in Greece. He moved to the United States at the age of nineteen and eventually settled in New Orleans. After living for a time in the West Indies and New York City, he moved to Japan in 1890. He became a Japanese citizen and a professor of English literature at the Imperial University of Tokyo.

Heckler, Melissa, reteller of "A House with a Star Inside," is a New York storyteller who has lived and worked with the Namibian Ju/'hoan Bushmen. She has been researching and telling their stories since 1981.

Leach, Maria, reteller of "The Soup Stone," is one of America's best-known folklorists. She is the compiler-editor of the *Standard Dictionary of Folklore, Mythology, and Legend* and other folklore collections for children and adults. A member of the American Folklore Society, of which she has been a Councilor, Leach lives in Nova Scotia.

Lear, Edward (1812-1888), author of "The Owl and the Pussy-Cat," was an English painter and nonsense poet.

Lester, Julius, reteller of "The Knee-High Man," is a professor in the Department of Judaic and Near Eastern Studies at the University of Massachusetts. His recent books include *The Tales of Uncle Remus* and *More Tales of Uncle Remus. Long Journey Home: Stories from Black History* was a National Book Award finalist.

MacDonald, Margaret Read, reteller of "Grandfather Bear is Hungry" and "Kanji-jo, the Nestlings," is a professional storyteller, children's librarian, and author. She wrote *The Storyteller's Sourcebook* and many books of stories, including *Twenty Tellable Tales* and *Look Back and See.*

Milne, A. A. (1882-1956), author of "Eeyore Has a Birthday and Gets Two Presents," was an English storyteller, poet, and dramatist.

Moroney, Lynn, author of "How the Stars Came to Be," is an Oklahoma storyteller/author with Chicasaw ancestry. She has recorded a tape of American Indian Star Tales entitled *The Feather Moon.* Her books include *Baby Rattlesnake, Elinda Who Danced in the Sky,* and *Coyote Dances with the Stars.*

Papashvily, George, and his wife, Helen, authors of "The Tale of the Tales," collected many Georgian folk tales in their book *Yes and No Stories.*

Paye, Won-Ldy, teller of "Why Leopard Has Black Spots," is from the Dan people of Liberia, where he was raised in a family of Griots—village storytellers and historians. In addition to being a storyteller, drummer, and actor, he directs a performing arts group in Seattle.

Simms, Laura, author of *The Squeaky Door,* is a professional storyteller for the American Museum of Natural History, the Hans Christian Andersen Society, and the New York Foundation for the Arts. *The Squeaky Door* is adapted from a Puerto Rican folk tale she heard told in Spanish in 1968.

Wolkstein, Diane, teller of "Squirrel's Song," is a professional storyteller. Some of her books include *The Magic Orange Tree* and *The Red Lion.*

Zemach, Margot, reteller of *It Could Always Be Worse,* has written and illustrated many children's books. *It Could Always Be Worse* received a *New York Times* Best Illustrated Children's Books of the Year award.

INDEX

Index of Literature by Origin

Africa
Hen and Frog (Hausa tale from Nigeria) 26
Kanji-jo, the Nestlings (Mende folk tale from West Africa) 42
Why Leopard Has Black Spots (Dan tale from Liberia) 88

Asia
The Foolish, Timid Rabbit (India) 66
The Old Woman Who Lost Her Dumplings (Japan) 72

British Isles
Eeyore Has a Birthday and Gets Two Presents (England) 119
Jack and the Beanstalk (England) 82
The Owl and the Pussy-Cat (England) 36

Eastern Europe
Grandfather Bear Is Hungry (Russia) 23
It Could Always Be Worse (Yiddish) 116
The Tale of the Tales (Russia) 131

North America
A Day When Frogs Wear Shoes 102
A House with a Star Inside 128
A Tall Turnip (Appalachian) 69
A Wolf and Little Daughter (African American) 79
How Our People Came to Be (Quechan story from the Southwest) 37
How the Stars Came to Be (Native American) 113
La Hormiguita (Spanish New Mexico) 32
Squirrel's Song (Hopi story from the Southwest) 16
The Black Cat (Eastern United States) 93
The Fox Went Out on a Chilly Night 64
The Knee-High Man (African American) 21
Turkey Makes the Corn and Coyote Plants It (White Mountain Apache) 39
Why Saguaros Grow on the South Side of Hills (Pima-Papago story from the Southwest) 38

Puerto Rico
The Squeaky Door 76

Scandinavia
The Emperor's New Clothes (Denmark) 51
The Wonderful Knapsack (Denmark) 58

Western Europe
Little Red Riding Hood (Germany) 55
The City Mouse and the Country Mouse (Greece) 111
The Elves and the Shoemaker (Germany) 100
The Soup Stone (Belgium) 108

Author and Storyteller Index

Aesop 111
Andersen, Hans Christian 51

Babbitt, Ellen C. 66
Baylor, Byrd 37
Bryan, Ashley 26

Cameron, Ann 102
Credle, Ellis 69

Ehrlich, Amy 51, 100
Erdoes, Richard 39

Grimm, Brothers 100

Hamilton, Virginia 79
Hatch, Mary C. 58
Haviland, Virginia 82
Hayes, Joe 32
Hearn, Lafcadio 72
Heckler, Melissa 128

Leach, Maria 108
Lear, Edward 36
Lester, Julius 21
Lippert, Margaret H. 55, 93

MacDonald, Margaret Read
    23, 42
Milne, A. A. 119
Moroney, Lynn 113

Ortiz, Alfonso 39

Papashvily, George and
    Helen 131
Paye, Won-Ldy 88

Simms, Laura 76

Wolkstein, Diane 16

Zemach, Margot 116

INDEX OF TITLES

Black Cat, The 93

City Mouse and the Country
  Mouse, The 111

Day When Frogs Wear Shoes,
  A 102

Eeyore Has a Birthday and Gets
  Two Presents 119
Elves and the Shoemaker,
  The 100
Emperor's New Clothes, The 51

Foolish, Timid Rabbit, The 66
Fox Went Out on a Chilly
  Night, The 64

Grandfather Bear Is Hungry 23

Hen and Frog 26
House with a Star Inside, A 128
How Our People Came to Be 37
How the Stars Came to Be 113

It Could Always Be Worse 116

Jack and the Beanstalk 82

Kanji-jo, the Nestlings 42
Knee-High Man, The 21

La Hormiguita 32
Little Red Riding Hood 55

Old Woman Who Lost Her
  Dumplings, The 72
Owl and the Pussy-Cat, The 36

Soup Stone, The 108
Squeaky Door, The 76
Squirrel's Song 16

Tale of the Tales, The 131
Tall Turnip, A 69
Turkey Makes the Corn and
  Coyote Plants It 39

Why Leopard Has Black Spots 88
Why Saguaros Grow on the
  South Side of Hills 38
Wolf and Little Daughter, A 79
Wonderful Knapsack, The 58

My Favorite Stories

MY FAVORITE STORIES

MY FAVORITE STORIES

My Favorite Stories